KU-675-552

# Thomas Chatterton

Garland Reference Library of the Humanities (Vol. 49)

By the same Author
in collaboration with H. A. Pausch

*Kommentierter Auswahlbibliographie zur Metaphorentheorie*, in
*Kommunikativ Metaphorik*, H. A. Pausch, ed. (Bonn: Bouvier, 1975)

# A Descriptive and Annotated
## Bibliography of
# Thomas Chatterton

## Murray Warren

*Garland Publishing, Inc., New York & London*

1977

Copyright © 1977
by Murray Warren

All Rights Reserved

**Library of Congress Cataloging in Publication Data**

Warren, Murray.
  A descriptive and annotated bibliography of
Thomas Chatterton.

  (Garland reference library of the humanities ;
v. 49)
  Includes index.
  1.  Chatterton, Thomas, 1752-1770--Bibliography.
I.  Title.
Z8163.W36  [PR3343]      016.821'6      75-42872
ISBN 0-8240-9951-6

*Printed in the United States of America*

TO

ALICE STORY

# ACKNOWLEDGEMENTS

This book presents bibliographical descriptions of separate publications and editions of the literary creations of Thomas Chatterton and of other authors' works in which a significant selection of Chatterton pieces is included, within the period from 1770 to 1803. This time span represents the formative years of the Chatterton canon. In addition to the descriptions I have prepared annotated check-lists of printed works classified under the following headings: 1) the Rowley Controversy; 2) Chatterton Biography: i. Books and Pamphlets and ii. Periodical Contributions from 1900; 3) Literary Criticism of Chatterton's Works; 4) Works of Imagination Based on Chatterton.

The original research for this bibliography was begun under the supervision of Professor George M. Story of the Department of English Language and Literature, Memorial University of Newfoundland, and it is to him that I owe my paramount indebtedness for his constructive criticism and calming reassurance.

I am deeply indebted, as well, to the patient and helpful librarians of the British Library, the Bristol Public Library, the Bodleian Library, Memorial University, and McGill University. In addition, I should like to thank the librarians of Harvard University, University of Illinois, Columbia University, University of Wisconsin, University of Chicago, Yale University, University of Texas, the Huntington Library, and the Chapin Library for the information they supplied regarding their copies of the 1772 edition of *The Execution of Sir Charles Bawdin*. My thanks also go to the British Library Board for their kind permission to reproduce photographs of the title pages of a number of the Library's Chatterton and other editions.

It would be extremely remiss of me not to mention a number of works that have been indispensable to the preparation of this bibliography, namely, *The Complete Works of Thomas Chatterton*, ed. D. S. Taylor and B. B. Hoover (Oxford, 1971); *Chattertoniana*, ed. F. A. Hyett and C. Bazeley (Gloucester, 1914); 'Thomas Chatterton, A Bibliography', in *A Bristol Bibliography*, ed. E. R. Norris (Bristol, 1916); and last, but by no means least, *Principles of Bibliographical Description*, by Professor Fredson T. Bowers (Princeton, 1949).

During the preparation of a work of this nature inevitably an author must call upon the assistance of many people for many reasons. Unfortunately, space does not permit me to thank by name each and every person who has helped in any way with the compilation of this bibliography; to them my gratitude is infinite.

*January, 1976.*                                                      **MURRAY   WARREN**

8

# C O N T E N T S

# ABBREVIATIONS

| | |
|---|---|
| A | *Athenaeum* |
| B | Bristol Public Library |
| Bk | *Bookman* |
| BMD | *Brittisches Museum für die Deutschen* |
| BMR | *British Magazine and Review* |
| BN&Q | *Bibliographical Notes and Queries* |
| BPL | Brighton Public Library |
| BT&M | *Bristol Times and Mirror* |
| CR | *Critical Review* |
| EM | *European Magazine* |
| EnR | *English Review* |
| ER | *Edinburgh Review* |
| G | *The Gazetteer* |
| GM | *Gentleman's Magazine* |
| GN&Q | *Gloucestershire Notes and Queries* |
| HD | Harvard College Library |
| itl. | italics |
| K-SJ | *Keats-Shelley Journal* |
| L | British Library, Reference Division |
| LD | Leeds University Library |
| LR | *London Review* |
| M | McGill McLennan Library |
| Meyerstein | *A Life of Thomas Chatterton* (London and New York, 1930) |
| mgn. nn. | marginal notes |
| MLN | *Modern Language Notes* |
| MLQ | *Modern Language Quarterly* |
| MLR | *Modern Language Review* |
| MM | *Monthly Magazine* |
| MMr | *Monthly Mirror* |
| MR | *Monthly Review* |
| N&Q | *Notes and Queries* |
| NB | *Neue Bibliothek der schönen Wissenschaften und der freyen Künste* |

| | |
|---|---|
| *NR* | *New Review* |
| *Nt* | *The Nation* |
| *O* | Bodleian Library, Oxford |
| *O¹* | St. Cross English Faculty Library, Oxford |
| *PBSA* | *Papers of the Bibliographical Society of America* |
| *PMLA* | *Papers of the Modern Language  Association* |
| *PQ* | *Philological Quarterly* |
| R. *or* rom. | Roman |
| *RES* | *Review of English Studies* |
| *RGL* | *Review and Guardian of Literature* |
| *SM* | *Scots Magazine* |
| *SR* | *Saturday Review* |
| *TLS* | *Times Literary Supplement* |
| *WDP* | *Western Daily Press*, Bristol |
| *YWES* | *Year's Work in English Studies* |

# List of Illustrations

# INTRODUCTION

## I. THOMAS CHATTERTON: LITERARY IMPOSTOR OR POET?

The phenomenon of literary imposture is ubiquitous, diverse and de-
fiant of precise definition. The famous 'Donation of Constantine', the pity-
seeking *Eikon Basilike* attributed to Charles I, William Lauder's accusations
against Milton and the bibliographical deceptions perpetrated by T. J. Wise
and Thomas Kirgate - all may be classed legitimately as examples of literary imposture despite the fact that each is of an entirely different nature.
The fabrication of imaginative literature, however, is a practice that did
not take hold until the eighteenth century.[1] Most celebrated among the 'gal-
lery of inventors' of the period are James Macpherson, William Henry Ireland
and, of course, Thomas Chatterton.

The eighteenth century revival of interest in mediaeval life and Go-
thic art and literature coincided with the foundation of serious Shakespear-
ean studies to play an important part in the establishment of a fanatical
search for antique literary treasures that was to last throughout most of the
period. The tantalising possibility that perhaps a great deal of work composed by or relating to writers of centuries past was still undiscovered brought about an antiquarian crusade dedicated to the rescue and preservation
of any literary artefact. There obviously existed a market for antique compositions and when the supply could not meet the demand, alternatives had to
be found. Macpherson, Ireland and Chatterton, among many others, obligingly

---

[1] Because the literary impostor appears in so many different disguises
- he may show himself as a fabricator of legal documents, as a printer of
spurious books, as a teller of false literary tales or as a creator of spurious literature - I shall, for the purposes of this study, restrict my attention to the mask worn by the impostor-poet. Therefore, when the term 'literary impostor' is hereafter employed, it is intended to mean one who con-
trives to pass off his own compositions as the work of someone else, usually
of a distant time and way of life.

provided them.[2]

That the fabrications of incompetent amateurs in the age of Gray, Warton and Johnson passed as authentic seems to us quite incredible, but one should bear in mind that during this period, perhaps more than at any other time in literary history, there existed a profoundly deep respect for things antique and rare. Eighteenth century antiquaries and lovers of literature quite reasonably assumed that since precious little was already known to exist in the way of an ancient literary heritage, more would ultimately come to light. Enthusiastic optimism blinded the less critical and it was usually to undiscriminating collectors that the impostor presented his 'discoveries'. Since none of the elaborate scientific apparatus used today to detect forged documents existed in the eighteenth century, the recipient of spurious material had only to rely on his intuition and previous experience, both of which were too often sadly deficient. Then when the 'discoveries' were denounced as forgeries, the original dupe and his supporters, for the most part merely to save face, obstinately maintained their first opinions that the documents in question were genuine. Usually the opponents in the resulting controversies became more interested in discrediting each other's arguments than in the object and the quarrel continued for its own sake. Those concerned allowed their initial belief, that the works before them were of considerable intrinsic merit, to be overshadowed by a ferocious debate on whether they were forgeries and their creator, after all, an impostor. Curious as those controversies may appear now, they do give the modern literary historian an intriguing insight into the workings of the critical mind of the period. When it was finally obvious they had been duped, eighteenth century scholars and critics inevitably reacted with moralising indignation, denouncing spurious literature as deserving no praise and little serious consideration. Unfortunately, those early denouncements have left their mark, encouraging critics, even today, to think of spurious literature as little more than an embarrassing phenomenon in the history of literary endeavour. Such is the case with

---

[2] The seemingly-endless list of eighteenth century literary impostors includes Charles Julius Bertram (1723-65), who produced a transcript of an alleged manuscript work by Richard of Cirencester and published the text of his forgery with a commentary on it at Copenhagen in 1757; Thomas Birch (1705-66), whose fabricated *Englishe Mercurie, imprinted at London by Her Highness's Printer, 1588*, appeared as England's earliest newspaper; Allan Cunningham

Thomas Chatterton's Rowley Poems.

It would be a mistake, however, to assume that posterity's attitude
to Chatterton as an impostor has remained rigidly unaltered since those early
days following his exposure. Closer examination of his standing in the eyes
of the literary world reveals a gradual, yet marked, change of attitude to
'the marvellous Boy'. Initial reaction to Chatterton was hostile in the extreme, but as time went by indignation was overtaken by the need to explain
logically, and thereby come to terms with, the character and behaviour of this
and all literary impostors. On the other hand, the literary world's assessment of Chatterton as a creator of legitimately imaginative literature has
not, until recently, seen significant development. Throughout the last two
centuries critics' interest in Chatterton and others of his ilk has focused,
not on their literary creations, but on the intriguing complexities of their
personalities. This bias towards the impostor's personality, as opposed to
the work he created, has for too long been fostered by a belief in the un-
written principle that spurious literature by its very nature lacks originality and authenticity and cannot, therefore, be regarded as truly creative.[3]
But by what criteria do we nominate the compositions of one man an outright
forgery, those of another a harmless hoax and of another 'legitimate literature'? Who is impostor and who creative artist? The absence of 'approved'
originality in an author's work may banish it from the realm of 'good' literature, that product of a mind whose creative talents and ideas are dependent
in large measure on its own native powers. Too frequently the critic's main
concern is to determine how and for what reasons the impostor perpetrated
his culpable act; that in the process he might have created legitimately imaginative literature is a possibility commonly ignored.

(1784-1842), who contributed much fabricated material to R. H. Cromek's *Remains of Nithsdale and Galloway Song*; John Jordan (1746-1809), whose tales
respecting Shakespeare are now believed to be fictitious; John Pinkerton
(1758-1826), who published his spurious *Select Scottish Ballads* in 1783; and
the colourful George Psalmanazar (1679?-1763), who delighted England with
his fabricated *Historical and Geographical Description of Formosa* in 1704.

[3] Admittedly, there were antiquaries who seemed most eager to extol
the excellence of the poems in the highest terms of applause, but the acclaim
was exclusively Rowley's, not Chatterton's. The supporters of Rowley refused
to entertain the possibility that a child of no account could have produced
poems so beautifully and so masterly.

In the period immediately following his suicide, Chatterton's contemporaries could find little sympathy for so daring an impostor. Thomas Warton was one of the first to speculate on the boy's motives for presenting his own writings as the creations of a fifteenth century monk, and for the most part, Warton's opinions are typical of the time:

> It will be asked, for what end or purpose did he contrive such an imposture? I answer, from lucrative views; or perhaps from the pleasure of deceiving the world, a motive which, in many minds, operates more powerfully than the hopes of gain. He probably promised himself greater emolument from this indirect mode of exercising his abilities: or, he might have sacrificed even the vanity of appearing in the character of an applauded original author, to the private enjoyment of the success of his invention and dexterity. [4]

Warton's suggestion that Chatterton's goals were mercenary and his motives devious embodied to a large extent the general opinion of many embarrassed antiquaries and literary dilettantes. If they had to admit being victims of a hoax, then it must have been instigated by one whose ambitions were founded in material greed and a perverted sense of moral honesty. The fact that they had been taken in by a young boy's crude fabrications disturbed a confidence in their ability to recognise the genuine and to expose the false. It was perhaps with a touch of intellectual snobbery, a feeling of injured pride and a desire for retribution that Warton concluded:

> It is with regret that I find myself obliged to pronounce Rowlie's poems to be spurious. Antient remains of English poetry, unexpectedly discovered, and fortunately rescued from a long oblivion, are contemplated with a degree of fond enthusiasm: exclusive of any real or intrinsic excellence, they afford those pleasures, arising from the idea of antiquity, which deeply interest the imagination. With these pleasures we are unwilling to part. But there is a more solid satisfaction, resulting from the detection of artifice and imposture. [5]

In spite of the recognition Warton and his contemporaries awarded Chatterton's impressive, if misguided, genius, the Rowley Poems lost all claims they might have had to the title of truly original creations simply because they were not the extraordinary antiques they purported to be. The critics' disappointment on realising that Chatterton's 'discoveries' were not the greatest single antiquarian rescue of the century, coupled with their desperate reluctance to relinquish all hope that a miraculous recovery of liter-

---

[4] *History of English Poetry* (London: J. Dodsley, 1778), II, p. 158.
[5] Warton, p. 164.

ary artefacts might yet occur, brought down on the Poems this harsh and dismissive verdict.

The publication of an account of the poet's short life in Sir Herbert Croft's *Love and Madness* (1780) initiated a more sympathetic opinion of Chatterton's case. It was Croft's view that the boy had been a frustrated, martyred, Werther-like genius whose treatment at the hands of his contemporaries, both before and after his death, had been nothing less than scandalous. This new champion of the young poet was later supported in his assessment by the Romantics; in fact, Blake, Wordsworth, Coleridge, Shelley and Keats admired and openly praised Chatterton's genius. To them he was the epitome of everything they believed and experienced as poetic artists: he had been deeply interested in antiquity and old poetry and legends; his was a frustrated attempt to gain recognition and respect in an unfeeling world; his poetic genius was more creative in the imaginary company of Rowley and Canynge than in the mercenary, uncouth streets of eighteenth-century Bristol; his youthful death symbolised the tragic fate that awaited so many striving young artists in their pursuit of spiritual Beauty and imaginative Truth; and perhaps most important, earlier critics had dismissed the Rowley Poems as curious examples of misguided creation whereas the Romantic poets maintained their source to be in Chatterton's powerful and purely imaginative genius. Blake's declaration, 'I believe both Macpherson and Chatterton, that what they say is Ancient Is so'[6], crystalises, in a sense, the fundamental Romantic principle that truly important Truths can only be expressed through an imagination that is uninhibited and pure. It is well known that the poetry of Wordsworth, Coleridge and Keats, in particular, was influenced by the Rowley Poems; however, it was the myth they created about the Bristol boy-poet that inspired them. The 'marvellous Boy' stanza in 'Resolution and Independence', Coleridge's 'Monody on the Death of Chatterton', and most strikingly, Keats' conception of the truly Romantic poet were inspired not so much by what Chatterton had written as by the circumstances of his life and death.

Among their fellow poets the Romantics won widespread support in their attempts to gain universal acceptance of the impostor-poet, but the

---

[6]
*Complete Writings*, ed. G. Keynes (Oxford University Press, 1969), p. 783.

general view in the early nineteenth century was that all who imposed on the credulity of the public were either criminals or victims of insanity and were regarded as dangerous individuals from whom society deserved protection. The unfortunate verdict of the inquest held into Chatterton's death was suicide by reason of insanity and this, coupled with Robert Southey's disclosure that the boy's sister had at one time been confined in a mental asylum and that he believed there had been a taint of madness in Chatterton himself[7], helped to form the general opinion that insanity not only caused the youth's untimely death but also drove him in his compulsion to forge poetry. Ironically, though, it was precisely this view that was instrumental in establishing an entirely new investigative approach to the character and behaviour of a literary impostor such as Chatterton.

By 1800 the developments in psychological investigation had progressed far enough to encourage some of the more adventurous critics to apply psychology's findings to their own interpretation of literature. For instance, Sir Walter Scott, in a review of the 1803 edition of Chatterton's works, offered a novel explanation of the impostor's personality. He disagreed with the rash judgment that Chatterton was actually insane; rather, Scott was of the opinion that the boy had been mentally unbalanced, a condition caused by 'that inequality of spirits with which Providence, as in mockery of the most splendid gifts of genius and fancy, has often conjoined them.'[8] It is clear from the review that Scott's concern was not primarily with the poems, some of which he ranked with 'the labours of our most distinguished poets', but with explaining, according to his understanding of contemporary psychology, the nature of Chatterton's personality and the motives for his deception. But Scott's attempts at literary psychoanalysis should by no means be misconstrued as a gesture of approval for the literary impostor; his final words leave no doubt as to his sentiments for one such as Chatterton who might presume to impose on the innocence of an unsuspecting public:

> The youthful reader, if conscious of powers which elevate him above his situation in life, may learn to avoid an overweening reliance upon his abilities, or an injurious and unfair exertion of them. He may learn, that if neglect or contempt obstruct him in the fair pursuit of fame, it is better to prefer obscurity, than to attain, by

[7] Letter to John Britton, 4 Nov. 1810, Bristol Public Library, MS. B20855.

[8] *ER*, 4 (1804), pp. 214-30.

the crooked path of literary forgery, the ambiguous reputation of an ingenious impostor. Above all, he may learn to guard against those sallies of an ill-regulated imagination, which buoyed up Chatterton with the most *unreasonable expectations*, only to plunge him into despair and suicide. And if there be one who, conscious of inferior mental powers, murmurs at being alloted but 'the single talent', and looks with envy on the flights of *superior genius*, let him read the life of Chatterton.[9]

Concern for the Chatterton dilemma led Robert Browning to write his vindication of the Bristol youth for insertion in the July 1842 issue of the *Foreign Quarterly Review*. In a bid to justify Chatterton's actions, Browning asserted that imitation is an instinct in all those who create for the first time; indeed, the development of genius is fed by the urge to imitate. As the prodigy matures his attempts at copying eventually give way to more original, creative efforts. Unfortunately, in Chatterton's case the imitative instinct assumed 'a proportionably bolder and broader shape' than is usual, and in consequence the natural inclination to produce original work found greater opposition than is normal. Unwarranted and unjustified was the common accusation that the boy's whole nature was 'one headstrong spirit of Falsehood'; in fact, 'he really made the most gallant and manly effort of which circumstances allowed to break through the sorry meshes that entangled him.'[10] It was to escape from the slavery of being merely the transcriber of Rowley, 'with no sentiment of his own which he might freely declare as such', that the boy finally decided to make his way to London and, hopefully, to a new life. As proof of Chatterton's resolve to break with the falseness of Rowley, to embark upon the road of Truth, even if it meant the pursuit of the lowest of all literary labours (hack-writing for magazines), Browning points out, 'We cannot conceive a more favourable field of enterprise than London would have afforded, had he been disposed to go on with the fabrication.'[11] As it turned out, Chatterton's desperately-sought freedom was to remain ever elusive, for no matter how hard he tried he could not ignore the power he possessed to impose upon innocent natures, and in the end, his moral effort triumphed over his intellectual one, and destroying the poems, he determined

---

[9] Scott. Italics are mine.

[10] *Essay on Chatterton*, ed. D. Smalley (Cambridge, Mass.: Harvard University Press, 1948), p. 120.

[11] Browning, p. 132.

to kill himself.

Browning's view of Chatterton's predicament is less an explicit statement of the facts than an imaginative speculation on the boy-poet's struggle
for self-determination. To vindicate the youth was Browning's intention, not
to offer an interpretation of the poetry; the significance of the Essay lies
in the more sympathetic and comprehensive treatment of Chatterton as a representative of literary impostors than had ever been advocated before.

The Essay's intimation that psychological forces had been responsible
for Chatterton's imposition acquired explicit statement some thirty years later by J. Addington Symonds. In his review of the 1871 edition of Chatterton's
poetical works, Symonds wrote:

> The termination of Chatterton's life illustrates [the] deeply seated
> duality of his nature. . . . The hypothesis of madness as an explan-
> ation of his suicide is but shallow. The psychologist discerns that
> the soul which had habituated itself morally and intellectually to a
> double existence, and had veiled its action in profoundest secrecy,
> could carry on the common concerns of life with interest to the verge
> of a calmly contemplated grave. [12]

At the time of this review the concept of 'split personality', arising from
a condition known generally as schizophrenia, had not been widely disseminat-
ed, but it was Symonds' identification of it with Chatterton's condition that
encouraged early twentieth century psychoanalytical studies of Bristol's 'marvellous Boy'.

Adlerian psychology induced Esther Ellinger, in her introduction to
Chatterton's satire, 'The Exhibition', to offer an interpretation of the boy-
poet's personality based on Adler's theory of the neurotic. According to
that eminent psychologist every individual struggles wilfully for the perfect-
ion of his personality, but occasionally an unconscious realisation that this
goal is in some way threatened leads to a form of anxiety known as 'the crav-
ing for security'. In the event that the neurotic should be unsuccessful in
achieving security, he may develop a defence mechanism to guard against any
possible degradation of personality. The mechanism is identifiable by symp-
toms characteristic of the condition: the subject may, through a 'will to
power', strive for a position of superiority in any situation where he feels

[12]*The Academy*, no. 38 (15 Dec. 1871), pp. 549-50.

threatened, he will tend to copy the mannerisms of grownups in order to real-
ise the privileges and dignity of adulthood, he may try to assert, however
unjustifiably, a prestigious ancestral background and he has a tendency to
belittle and degrade others through satire in order to heighten his own sense
of self-esteem.  In his desire to further his security the neurotic may even
attempt escape from hard or dull reality by fantasising a dream-world 'where
he achieves a second-hand security sufficient to bring relief from the pres-
sure of the actual.'[13]  In the final analysis the neurotic's propensity towards extreme abstemious habits may be regarded as 'a self-torturing exped-
ient whose purpose is to enhance the feeling of personal esteem, even at the
subject's own expense.  So occasionally he proceeds to devices of self-tor-
ture . . . the most abnormal of all attitudes, for it employs the martyr's
method of self-execration, and self-reproach; of self-castigation even to the
length of suicide.'[14]

Miss Ellinger believes that Chatterton matches accurately Adler's
picture of the neurotic.  The Bristol boy-poet had the ability to become
master of any situation whether it be with his young companions at Colston's
Charity School or with the Barretts and Catcotts of the city's older gener-
ation.  He was very often described as a boy too mature for his years; in
fact, he tended to prefer the company of adults with whom he felt more at
ease.  He went to great lengths to support his unfounded claims to a noble
ancestry.  Poems such as 'The Exhibition' frequently embody scathing and
vindictive attacks on those who had done most to help him.  The creation of
Rowley was a means of escape from the mundane lessons at Colston's and the
boring duties of his apprenticeship at Lambert's, the lawyer.  And finally,
the many reports that the boy had often deprived himself of food and sleep
in order to carry on his 'work', the letter to Barrett after the discovery
of his intention to commit suicide (for which the only excuse he could offer
was his 'damn'd native, inconquerable Pride') and the desperate act that in
the end released him from his torment - all these add up to a convincing
case that Chatterton was, indeed, suffering from severe neurosis.  It is


[13]
    *Thomas Chatterton, The Marvelous Boy* (Philadelphia: University of
Pennsylvania Press, 1930), p. 40.
[14]
    Ellinger.

Miss Ellinger's intention to show how Adler's theories offer an appropriate framework to the biographer's picture of Chatterton and to propose a plausible alternative explanation for the creation of Rowley and the poems Chatterton claimed were antique.

As if not to be outdone by the Adlerians the Freudians have also made their mark in the field of Chatterton criticism. They claim that imposture arises from a situation in which the normal processes leading up to the Oedipal conflict and its eventual resolution are in some way obstructed. In a series of papers dealing with imposture and the artist Phyllis Greenacre promoted the theory that due to the absence of the father, either because of death or desertion, the child is frustrated in his attempts at overcoming the Oedipal conflict and the resulting imbalance in the Oedipal relationship encourages the future impostor towards an intense maternal attachment. This overweening reliance on his mother arrests the normal development of the subject's personality and his sense of a separate self is thereby undermined. The child is thus forced to create another, more independent personality in order to overcome his feelings of helplessness and incompleteness. [15] Among Miss Greenacre's list of famous impostors Thomas Chatterton's name figures prominently: had he not been born a posthumous child, the father having died almost four months before his son's birth? Did not the boy exhibit an excessive fondness for his mother and his sister? Was not the mask of Rowley worn in a fruitless search for his own misplaced identity? Miss Greenacre's theory, though written primarily for other psychologists, offers the student of Chatterton yet another interpretation of the literary impostor phenomenon.

Literary history's fixation with the 'psychology' of Chatterton has almost entirely overshadowed the need for a just and adequate assessment of the merits of the Rowley Poems. Until the 1930's the attention Chatterton attracted was inevitably aroused by the circumstances of his life and death; very little interest was shown in the Rowley Poems per se. The one scholar and devotee of Chatterton who did more than any other in the first decades of this century to illuminate with competence the details of the poet's brief life and to awaken a literary interest in the remarkable nature of the Rowley Poems was E. H. W. Meyerstein. His *Life of Thomas Chatterton* is an indispens-

[15] 'The Impostor', *Psychoanalytic Quarterly*, 17 (1958), pp. 359-82.

ble guide to any study of the 'marvellous Boy' and the section dealing with
the Rowley Poems (pp. 156-249) is one of the all-too-few introductions avail-
ble to the new reader. The nature of his study permitted Meyerstein but a
superficial critical examination of the Poems, yet his observations are acute.
From the *Life* one learns of the historical sources from which Chatterton drew
his characters and events, of the reference material he possibly employed to
construct his pseudo- Middle English and of the influence of Spenserian pro-
sody on the Poems. Included as well are comments on Chatterton's debt to
Shakespeare and Dryden and a brief exposition on the Poem's imagery.

Regrettably, apart from Meyerstein's contributions to Chatterton criticism and the recent excellent edition of the complete works[16], the number of
attempts at interpreting the Rowley Poems are far fewer than one might reasonably expect. Among the more significant contributions are two studies by
Bertrand H. Bronson: in the first he views Elizabeth Cooper's *The Muses' Library* (1737) as a major source of inspiration for the poems; in the second he
treats Rowley as a 'father figure' in Chatterton's development as a writer.[17]
Robert Gittings pursues a profitable line by considering Chatterton's influence on Keats' poetry[18]; his work is supplemented by a contribution from Nai-
tung Ting.[19] W. Macneile Dixon makes a valuable study of the poet's work a-
gainst the background of the mediaeval revival.[20] And Donald S. Taylor dis-
cusses the chronology of the Rowley Poems, questioning established opinions
and exploring new ideas in order to place more accurately each work within
the short life-span of the poet's career.[21] These contributions are valuable
additions to a greater understanding and appreciation of Chatterton's spurious
compositions, but their numbered few should in no way be taken as a reflect-
ion of the Poem's intrinsic merits.

It would seem, then, that the appalling lack of attention to the Rowley

[16] *The Complete Works of Thomas Chatterton*, eds. D. S. Taylor and B. B.
Hoover (Oxford at the Clarendon Press, 1971).
[17] 'Chattertoniana', *MLQ*, 11 (1950), pp. 417-24; *Thomas Chatterton* (New
Haven: Yale University Press), 1949.
[18] 'Keats and Chatterton', *K-SJ*, 4 (1955), pp. 47-54.
[19] 'The Influence of Chatterton on Keats', *Ibid.*, 5 (1956), pp. 103-08.
[20] *Chatterton* (Warton Lecture on English Poetry from *Proceedings of the
British Academy*, 1930).
[21] 'Chatterton: The Problem of Rowley Chronology and its Implications',
*PQ*, 46 (1967), 268-76.

Poems is the result chiefly of two factors: on the one hand, the 'myth' of the boy-poet Chatterton has for two centuries fascinated literary historians and has drawn their interest steadily away from his remarkable compositions, and on the other, the literary world has never considered spurious literature meritous of prolonged and detailed analysis. As regards the Rowley Poems, the influence of these unfortunate circumstances has been eradicated to some extent with the appearance of Meyerstein's *Life* and the recent edition of Chatterton's works, so that, apart from our traditional prejudices, there is nothing to hinder our accepting the Rowley Poems as legitimately imaginative creations worthy of far more than a cursory glance.

Ours is an uncomplimentary attitude to the author of the Rowley Poems, and on an even larger scale we exhibit a universal ignorance of the creations of impostor-poets. Chatterton's neglect as a legitimate poet is sadly shared by other authors who chose, for whatever reason, to pass off their compositions as those of another. Surely it is time to re-assess our attitudes to impostor-poets and recognise the glaring incongruities in our sense of values when we are confronted with what we have come to know, for want of a better term, as 'spurious literature'.

## II. EXPLANATION OF THE BIBLIOGRAPHY

The purposes of this bibliography are manifold; that is, it attempts o present bibliographical descriptions of early Chatterton editions (includng selections of Chatterton in other authors' works) dating from 1770 to 803, as well as annotated check-lists of printed works dealing with the Powey controversy, Chatterton biography, literary criticism of his works, and vorks of imagination based on Chatterton.

I have described only those editions published between 1770 and 1803 or two reasons: 1) the formative period of the Chatterton canon occurs beween those years, *i.e.*, the first separate publication of a Chatterton work admittedly, now considered to be of doubtful authenticity) appeared in 1770 and the first attempt to collect within a single edition all of Chatterton's rose and poetry took place in 1803; and 2) all of the numerous Chatterton ditions published after 1803 (except for the 1971 Oxford edition of the *Jorks*) are derivative; that is, they are reprints of some former edition and herefore offer limited or no textual authority. Even within the period 1770 o 1803 there are not many instances where a single edition provides complete extual authority (this is made obvious in the 1971 edition), but the importance of those editions as representatives of the development of the Chatteron canon should not be taken too lightly. It is my hope that the descriptons hereafter provided will assist librarians, collectors, and Chatterton scholars alike to identify with some degree of certainty any of the early hatterton editions that may fall under their scrutiny.

The descriptions, with the three exceptions noted presently, are aranged according to a chronological sequence beginning with the 1772 edition of *The Execution of Sir Charles Bawdin* and continuing until the 1803 Southey nd Cottle edition of the *Works*.[1] Two works, Barrett's *History of Bristol* and regory's *Life of Chatterton*, were published in the same year, but since no recise date of publication for either is known, they have been arranged alhabetically according to the surname of the author. I have placed the

[1] In one instance only has it been necessary to guess at the date of ublication of an edition, namely, the second *Supplement to the Miscellanies: 'Kew Gardens'*. Unfortunately, only a single copy of this edition is known to xist and that lacks the title leaf.

description of the 1799 edition of the *Rowley Poems* immediately after that
for 1794 because the former is a re-issue, with a cancel title-leaf, of the
latter and is, except for the title, identical to it in every respect. The
1770 editions of *The Elegy to William Beckford* and *The Auction* are considered
to be of doubtful authenticity[2], and the descriptions of them are placed
under the heading of 'Dubia', and after that for 1803.

In cases where one edition is almost an exact reprint of another,
with only minor variations (*e.g.*, the second 1777 and the 1778 *Rowley Poems*
are both almost exact reprints of the first 1777 edition, and the 1799 *Rowley Poems* is, apart from the title-leaf, a re-issue of 1794), or where only
a selection of Chatterton pieces is found in another author's work or in an
editor's collection, the descriptions are given in an abbreviated form, particularly as regards the listing of contents.

The descriptions begin with a separate heading (in bold type), each
prefixed by its number, and consisting of the surname of the author (if not
Chatterton) or editor, the short title of the edition, the place of publication, the name of the publisher, and the date of publication, if any or all of
these are known. In some cases a number of descriptions, particularly those
of editions about which something more than the obvious is known or concerning which some discussion has been raised by Chatterton scholars, are prefixed by introductory notes discussing a variety of special matters relating
to their history.

Then follows a quasi-facsimile transcript of half- and full-title
pages[3], with any variant forms given immediately afterwards in square brackets.

---

[2]Meyerstein's acceptance of the Beckford elegy (*Life*, p. 382) and his
arguments for Chatterton's authorship of *The Auction* (*Life*, pp. 383-86) are
countered by D. S. Taylor, 'The Authenticity of Chatterton's *Miscellanies in
Prose and Verse*', PBSA, 55 (1961), pp. 289-96 and in his edition of the *Works*
(Oxford, 1971, 2, pp. 789-90 and 1150-51). One of the points of Taylor's
argument against Chatterton's authorship of the Beckford elegy is that 'it is
generally Patriotic rather than specifically Chattertonian in tone, diction,
and allusions'. It is perhaps worth noting here that in his letter to Thomas
Cary, dated 1 July 1770 (only ten days after Beckford's death), Chatterton
complained, 'The Printers of the Daily Publications are all frightened out of
their Patriotism, and will take Nothing unless tis Moderate or Ministerial, I
have Not had five Patriotic Essays this fortnight. All must be Ministerial or
Entertaining.' (Oxford *Works*, 1, p. 642).

[3]In the case of the 1794 *Rowley Poems* and its 1799 re-issue, a quasi-
facsimile transcript of the engraved title precedes that of the full-title.
For the convenience of the reader an illustration of the engraved title is
provided.

Should any edition consist of more than one volume, a transcript of the half-
and full-title pages of the first volume only is given, but variants in subsequent volumes are noted immediately afterwards in square brackets. In one
case (Anderson, *The Works of the British Poets*, 1794, 95), a transcript of
the volume title is provided and this is followed by a transcript of the
title to the Chatterton selection.[4]

Type styles are imitated as far as the limitations of a typewriter
will allow, that is, roman and italic type are followed in the transcript,
but black-letter is indicated thus: The Works. Two sizes of type (or the
large and small capitals of a fount) in the same line are distinguished by
the use of a solid line below those letters which are smaller. Thus, in
the word CHURCH, all the underlined letters are small capitals, while the initial letter is a full capital. The roman long-s is reproduced thus: ſ, and
the italic long-s thus: ſ. Ligatures and digraphs are indicated thus: ftay,
Ælla. The roman and italic ampersand are distinguished and reproduced as
accurately as possible. If a word has to be divided at the end of a line,
it is not given a hyphen unless the original happens to be hyphenated at the
same point.

Where colophons are present, these are reproduced in quasi-facsimile
directly after the transcript of the title page. Should a colophon be located at the bottom of a page carrying the text (as opposed to being located
on an otherwise blank page), this fact is denoted by reference to its location as 'on M4$^b$'.

In the collation the format of the edition is identified, followed
by the collational formula. The occurence of the Greek letter $\pi$ in square
brackets at the beginning of a formula denotes the presence of a prefixed
unsigned leaf or gathering. Similarly, the Greek letter $\chi$ is used for an unsigned and uninferred leaf or gathering which is not prefixed. When the signing begins with signature b, *b*, B, or *B* and there is an unsigned prefixed
gathering, or separate leaves, the inferential signature a, *a*, A, or *A* is supplied in square brackets. When two or more duplicated signature alphabets
follow each other in regular sequence, I have shortened a formula such as
$-Z^8$ Aa-Zz$^8$ Aaa-Zzz$^8$ to A-3Z$^8$. Thus, when the signature 3T8 is used, it is

[4]In this instance it has been necessary to break the line-for-line
continuous transcript of both titles and to reproduce the letterpress set
in triple or double columns.

meant to refer to the eighth leaf of the third T-gathering, or Ttt8. When signature alphabets are duplicated in the same fount (*e.g.*, B–L$^8$ B–S$^8$), the second series is prefixed by a superior or index figure, thus: B–L$^8$ $^2$B–S$^8$. Then signature $^2$D3 will refer to the third leaf of the gathering signed B in the second series of alphabetical signatures of the same fount. The use of a ± sign in association with a specific signature (*e.g.* ±c4) indicates that that leaf is a signed cancellans.

The collational formula is followed by a statement of signing, in square brackets, so that [$4 (–a4, +D5) signed] means that normally the first four leaves of every gathering are signed, except that leaf a4 is unsigned and leaf D5 is specially signed. After the statement of signing the number of leaves (exclusive of binder's blanks and inserted plates) is given, followed by the statement of pagination. Parts of a pagination sequence which are missing, but which can be inferred, are supplied in italics without brackets, while any unnumbered pages not included in the printer's own complete system of numeration are noted by italicized total in square brackets. This is followed by a statement, in square brackets, of missigning, misnumbering, incorrect positioning of a number, and a list of all unnumbered pages that one would expect normally to be numbered.

The list of contents comes after the collation and the method of transcription is the same as that used for the title page. Superscript italic letters (*a* or *b*) refer to the recto or verso of a particular leaf; thus, A2$^a$ is the recto of the second leaf of gathering-A. Where head-titles are present these are reproduced in quasi-facsimile and their locations noted. Only a selection of the running-titles is given, particularly those which contain variants. First, the running-title is reproduced in quasi-facsimile (a vertical stroke separating two parts of a running-title indicates that the first part is located on the verso of one leaf and the second part on the recto of the following leaf); its location is then noted. Should any variants of the normal running-title occur, these and their locations are noted in square brackets. Catchwords are reproduced in quasi-facsimile with the location of the catchword given first, followed by the catchword itself, and then its variant form in square brackets as it appears at the beginning of the next page.

The section concerned with typography has as its first item the number

f lines of ordinary text on a typical full page, with the location of the
age measured in brackets after it. The measurement, in millimeters, of
he length of the lines of letterpress is given, followed in brackets by
he measurement of the overall type-page, from the top of the headline type
o the bottom of the direction-line, and this, in turn, is followed by the
idth of the type-page. The measurement of twenty lines of continuous type
s stated and the type, whether roman, italic or black-letter is identified,
o that 112R. means that twenty lines of continuous roman type measures 112
illimeters. Should the text also contain verse, the maximum width of type
f a line of verse is stated and the location of the page measured is noted
n brackets after it.

In cases where press figures are present the various numbers and their
ocations are given. Plates are located and described briefly and the length
nd width of the plate-marks are given in brackets.

Whenever matters relating to the textual and printing history of an
dition are not extensive enough to warrant the creation of a special intro-
uction at the beginning of the description, such matters are dealt with in
he notes at the end of the description. Included here are records of the
ppearance for the first time of any Chatterton **piece** not collected or print-
d before, a statement (when it can be determined) of the derivation of any
articular edition, plus any subsequent reprints thereof, the occurence of
anuscript notes and when known, the writers thereof, plus collections of
hattertoniana, found in individual copies examined, a record of publication
nnouncements, the occurence of peculiarities such as double title-leaves,
rinting marks on titles, and inserted leaves, the measurement of an engraved
evice on a title page, and the appearance of decorative head- and tail-pieces.

When the publication of contemporary reviews of an edition is known,
heir locations are noted in a special section devoted to this purpose.

Finally, the description ends with the location and the shelf-marks
f individual copies examined.

The Rowley controversy got underway shortly after Chatterton's death
nd continued even into the present century, so to record every contribution
o that often heated debate would require more space than can conveniently be
llowed here. Therefore, I have included in the check-list only books, pam-
hlets, and periodical contributions up to and including 1882 (by which time
he matter of the authenticity of the Rowley Poems had been settled for all

but a few die-hards). The entries have been alphabetically arranged according to the surname of the author and where there is more than one work by the same writer, the entries are arranged alphabetically according to the title of the work. I should point out that all the periodical contributions have been assembled under the letter 'P' for Periodicals and arranged alphabetically according to the title of the magazine. Where there is more than one article from the same magazine, the entries are arranged chronologically.

The check-list of Chatterton biography is divided into two sections: 1) Books and Pamphlets, and 2) Periodicals. The first section has its entries arranged alphabetically according to the authors' surnames and where more than one work appears by the same writer, the entries are arranged alphabetically according to title. The second section has been arranged according to the surname of the contributor and I have limited the check-list only to contributions published after 1900. When more than one article appears under the same author, they are arranged alphabetically according to the title of the piece.

Literary criticism of Chatterton's works has been so neglected that it is possible in a relatively short space to include virtually every contribution to that aspect of Chatterton scholarship. The entries are arranged according to the surname of the author and where more than one title appears under the same writer, the entries are again arranged alphabetically according to the title of the work.

The scope of the last check-list, dealing with works of imagination based on Chatterton, has been, perhaps, the most difficult one to limit. I have included only those works that are based entirely on Chatterton, and for this reason, regrettably, I have had to exclude some of the best known references to Chatterton. For example, Wordsworth's famous 'marvellous Boy' stanza from 'Resolution and Independence' will not be found in the check-list, principally because the entire poem is not itself based on Chatterton. The entries are arranged alphabetically according to the surname of the author and where more than one work is by the same writer, the entries are arranged alphabetically according to the title of the work.

EARLY EDITIONS, 1770 - 1803

# 1. THE EXECUTION OF SIR CHARLES BAWDIN (LONDON: F. NEWBERY, 1772)

The editor of *The Execution* has been identified as Thomas Eagles in
a letter dated 8 May 1772 from Dr. Francis Woodward to George Catcott.[1] The
edition shows no consistent pattern of agreement with any of the three extant
manuscripts at *B*: B.5344 (Catcott); B.6493 (Thomas Fry); B.20928 (unknown
hand).

Following R. W. Chapman's having raised a point in the collation of
*The Execution* (*Bibliographical Notes & Queries*, 2 (1935), p. 8), P. H. Muir
offered the following explanation:

> The first edition exists with two title-pages, one with the im-
> print of W. Goldsmith, the other with that of F. Newbery. Copies
> are known with both title-pages. Mr. Chapman's copy, with the
> Newbery imprint, is uncut, but lacks the last leaf, H1, paged 25-
> 26. He had surmised that the title-leaf and H were printed to-
> gether and folded round the rest. In point of fact, a copy with
> the Goldsmith imprint, also uncut, shows that both the title-leaf
> and the last leaf - H - are inserts, which seems to indicate that
> the two titles were printed together and that occasionally one or
> the other of the two publishers omitted to remove the title-page
> with his rival's imprint.[2]

As it turns out, Muir's explanation is entirely erroneous. On closer
examination of the two British Library copies containing both titles, I noticed
that the distance between the chain-lines of the Goldsmith title measures 26mm.,
while the distance between the chain-lines of the Newbery title and of all the
other leaves is 31mm. Goldsmith's title, therefore, is an insert.

If, as Chapman suspected, the Newbery title leaf and the H-leaf are
conjugate, the indented side of each leaf will match (*i.e.* if the recto of the
title leaf is indented, the verso of H1 is the matching indented side, and *vice
versa*). Of the copies with the Newbery title I have examined (two in all), the

[1]Meyerstein, p. 451.

[2]'A Chatterton Edition', *TLS* (5 April 1941), p. 172.

33

indented side of the title leaf matches that of H1.[3]

It would seem, then, that it was Newbery who was the original publisher, since it is his imprint that is most probably conjugate with H1, and
that title leaves for Goldsmith were later printed and used to cancel the
Newbery title. In some cases, though, Goldsmith omitted to remove his rival's
title and consequently some copies containing both titles reached the book-
sellers.

*The Execution* was reprinted as a separate publication by the Bristol
School of Printing at the Merchant Venturers' Technical College, Bristol, in
1932.

[3]Librarians at the Chapin Library and at Columbia and Yale Universit-
ies inform me that in their copies of *The Execution* the indented side of the
Newbery title matches that of H1.

Fig. Ia. Title page of *The Execution of Sir Charles Bawdin* (Newbery Imprint), 1772

Fig. Ib. Title page of *The Execution of Sir Charles Bawdin* (Goldsmith Imprint), 1772

THE | EXECUTION | OF | Sir CHARLES BAWDIN. | DEDICATED | TO HER GRACE
THE | DUTCHESS OF NORTHUMBERLAND. | *Durat Opus Vatum.* | LONDON: | Sold
by F. NEWBERY, the Corner of ST. PAUL'S CHURCH-YARD. | MDCCLXXII. |
[Price Two Shillings and Sixpence.]

[*Second title:* as above except 'Sold by W. GOLDSMITH, at No. 20, PATER-
NOSTER-ROW.' instead of 'Sold by F. NEWBERY, the Corner of ST. PAUL'S
CHURCH-YARD.'; identical type-setting]

*Collation:* 4° in 2s. [π]¹ [A]² B–G² H¹ [$1 (−π1, A1) signed]; 16 leaves,
pp. [2] *i-iii* iv, 1-26.

*Contents:* π1ᵃ: title (verso blank); A1ᵃ: 'TO HER GRACE | ELIZABETH, | DUTCH
ESS OF NORTHUMBERLAND, | IN HER OWN RIGHT | BARONESS PERCY, LUCY, POYN
INGS FITZ-PAYNE, | BRYAN, AND LATIMER, | BEHIND WHOSE ILLUSTRIOUS NAME |
THE RELIQUES | OF | ANCIENT ENGLISH POETRY | WERE WITH PROPRIETY INTRO
DUCED INTO THE WORLD, | THIS PIECE | IS WITH ALL HUMILITY DEDICATED | BY
THE EDITOR.' (verso blank); A2ᵃ: 'PREFACE.'; B1ᵃ: 'THE | EXECUTION | OF |
Sir CHARLES BAWDIN.'

HT] THE | EXECUTION | OF | Sir CHARLES BAWDIN.    B1ᵃ

RT] PREFACE.    A4ᵇ
THE EXECUTION OF | SIR CHARLES BAWDIN.    B1ᵃ-H1ᵃ [THE EXECUTION OF, &c.
H1ᵇ]

CW] E1ᵃ L. Yett [L. | "Yett]

*Typography:* 20 ll. (B2ᵇ), 130(170) x 96mm., 130R.

*Notes:* 1.Copies containing both titles: L (C.39.h.20; Ashley 2804); all other
copies contain the Goldsmith title only.

2. Publication announcements: *GM*, 42 (June 1772), p. 285: 'The Execution
of Sir Charles Bawdin. Dedicated to her Grace the Dutchess of Northumberland. 4to. 2s.6d. Goldsmith'; from a copy of the third edition of the
*Rowley Poems* (ed. Tyrwhitt, 1778) a paste-in with no record of the magazine
where nor the date when the announcement appears: 'To the Admirers of Antient Poesy, *This Day was published, Price 2s. 6d.* Dedicated to her Grace
the Duchess of Northumberland, The Execution of Sir Charles Bawdin. Attributed to Thomas Rowlie, a Priest, in the fifteenth century. "Durat opus
vatum". Printed for W. Goldsmith, No. 20, Paternoster row.' *O* (Douce.C.244).

*Reviewed:* CR, 34 (Sept. 1772), pp. 234-36.

*Copies examined:* L (C.39.h.20; Ashley 2804; 11632.g.38; C.59.f.26; CUP.400.e.3);
B (B.5343; B.11066).

## 2. ROWLEY POEMS (LONDON: T. PAYNE & SON, 1777; 1ST. EDN.)

The first editor of the Rowley Poems was a contemporary of Chatterton, Thomas Tyrwhitt (1730-86). His early interest in the Poems was eloquently expressed in an edition of *The Canterbury Tales*:

> The influence of those malignant stars, which so long confined poor Rowley in his iron chest, seems still to predominate. Seriously it were much to be wished, that the gentleman, who is possessed of the still remaining fragments of this unfortunate author, would print them as soon as possible. If he should not have the leisure or inclination to be the Editor he might easily find a proper person to take that trouble for him as nothing would be more requisite, than to print the several pieces from their respective MSS. distinguishing which of those MSS. are original and which are transcripts, and also by whom, and when the transcripts were made, as far as that can be ascertained.[1]

The person most instrumental in the realization of Tyrwhitt's wishes for publication was one Dr. Francis Woodward who acted as the mediator between the parties involved. Woodward approached George Symes Catcott, a recipient of many of the poet's earlier fabrications, in January 1776 to sound out the latter's views on the possible publication of the poems. From the outset Catcott, who firmly believed in the poems' authenticity, encouraged the venture, indicating to Woodward that he would be willing to consider surrendering copies of his collection of the Rowley Poems to a reputable editor. Acting on this encouragement Woodward, with the assistance of Thomas Crofts, chaplain to the Duke of Leeds, inquired of Tyrwhitt and Thomas Payne, the London publisher and bookseller, whether they might be interested in bringing the poems to print.

In February Catcott forwarded to Tyrwhitt copies of his entire collection and for them Payne paid him fifty guineas.[2] On 27 April of that year Tyrwhitt informed Catcott, 'The Poems are in the Press and I should hope will be ready for Publication in the course of the next winter.'[3]

---

[1]*The Canterbury Tales of Chaucer* (London, 1775), 3, p. 318.

[2]Meyerstein, pp. 450*ff*.

[3]From a letter quoted in L. F. Powell's 'Thomas Tyrwhitt and the *Rowley Poems*', *RES*, 7 (July 1931), p. 317.

Meanwhile, the other possessor of Chatterton's 'originals', William Barrett, a Bristol surgeon and antiquary, could not be persuaded to part with his share of Chattertoniana. He was in the midst of preparing his *History of Bristol* and among the material he had received from Chatterton were fragments relating to the Canynge family, well-known ancestors of the city of Bristol. Believing in the historic accuracy of the pieces Barrett intended that they should first reach the public eye in his *History*.

Growing scepticism about the authenticity of the Poems and the Johnson-Boswell visit to Bristol and their subsequent verdict that the productions were, indeed, of a spurious nature, began to sow seeds of doubt in Tyrwhitt's mind. Until that point he appears to have been convinced of the poems' genuineness. Six months after the purchase of Catcott's copies and four months after they had gone to press, Tyrwhitt and George Steevens, who had offered his assistance in editing the poems, finally went to Bristol (August 1776) to see the original manuscripts for themselves. Upon their arrival a meeting with Barrett was arranged and the following agreement, according to a letter from Catcott to Dean Jeremiah Milles dated 28 May 1777, was arrived at:

> Mr Tyrwhitt printed one Sheet of Turgot's History [sold to him by Catcott], and intended compleating it, as also the Account of great Men . . . born in Bristol, but afterwards at Mr. Barrett's desire, suppressed all the Prose MSS. because they shd. not interfere with his Publication.[4]

In return Tyrwhitt received 'English Metamorphosis', 'The Battle of Hastings, No. 2', 'Epitaph on Robert Canynge', part of 'The Storie of William Canynge' and 'The Accounte of W. Canynges Feast'.

As a consequence of his visit to Bristol, Tyrwhitt altered his edition and the changes were later reported by John Nichols (*Illustrations*, 1817):

> Mr. Tyrwhitt was actually a *believer* when he first printed on the subject; but, seeing good ground for changing his opinion, he actually canceled several leaves before his volume was published.[5]

The only cancel distinguishable in the copies I have examined is the leaf c4, containing the Advertisement:

> *THE Reader is desired to observe, that the notes at the bottom*

[4]Powell, p. 322.
[5]Powell, p. 323.

37

*of the several pages, throughout the following part of this book, are all copied from MSS. in the hand-writing of* Thomas Chatterton.

Of the copies examined, *B* (B.5194) and *O* (Vet.A5.e.2122) contain the original unsigned c4-leaf with the reading, '*THE Reader is desired . . . in the hand-writing of* Thomas Chatterton, *and were probably composed by him.*'[6]

The cancellation of the original Advertisement leaf is testimony to the fact that Tyrwhitt wished to remain as impartial as possible on the question of authenticity. In the preface (p. xii) he declares:

> Whatever may have been [Chatterton's] part in [the 'extraordinary transaction']; whether he was the author, or only the copier (as he constantly asserted) of all these productions; he appears to have kept the secret entirely to himself, and not to have put it in the power of any other person, to bear certain testimony either to his fraud or to his veracity.

In the light of this situation Tyrwhitt concludes that only a thorough examination of the existing vellum manuscripts and *all* the internal evidence could establish with any degree of certainty whether the Poems were authentic. In the event that those fragments purporting to be historic artefacts should be proved genuine, it would 'still remain to be determined, how far their genuineness should serve to authenticate the rest of the collection, of which no copies, older than those made by Chatterton [had] been produced' (p. xii). If, on the other hand, 'the writing of the Fragments . . . be counterfeit and forged by Chatterton, it [would] not necessarily follow, that the matter of them was also forged by him, and still less, that all the other compositions, which he professed to have copied from antient MSS., were merely inventions of his own' (pp. xii-xiii). Whether rightly or wrongly, Tyrwhitt did not feel it his duty as an editor to decide the question of authenticity; that task he preferred tactfully 'to leave . . . to the determination of the unprejudiced and intelligent Reader.'

[6]Positive proof of the cancellation has been determined from the following evidence: i) the cancellans is signed in a larger type fount than that employed for the other two signatures of the gathering; ii) an irregular stub is visible between c3 and c4; iii) the chain-indentations of the cancellans do not match those of halfsheet c. *O* (2799.e.288) is wanting c4, but part of the Advertisement can be seen offset on the verso of c3 and clearly it, too, represented the cancellandum.

As for the cancellation of the whole *sheets* mentioned by Nichols, R. W. Chapman points out that it is 'a process which can be completed at once; and if Tyrwhitt really executed a *volte-face* at the last moment, he would naturally take what precautions he could.'[7] Whether such whole-scale cancellation actually did take place is a matter for conjecture; as yet no evidence has come to light that in any way supports Nichols' assertion.

A pre-publication printing of the preliminaries (sigs. $b1^a$ to $c4^a$) appeared in the *Annual Register*, 19 (1776), Antiquities: pp. 155-62 and the edition itself was published on Saturday, 8 February 1777. Of the twenty-six pieces found therein, ten were printed directly from manuscripts in Chatterton's handwriting, whereas the remainder were derived from copies thereof: ten were printed from George Catcott's copies of the poet's manuscripts; one from a Barrett copy of a Chatterton holograph; two from previously printed sources (one of which was corrected from a Catcott copy); two from transcripts made by Tyrwhitt of manuscripts in Barrett's possession; and one from the editor's copy of the first thirty-four lines of a manuscript owned by Barrett. The remaining one was printed from a Catcott copy, corrected from another in Barrett's hand.

[7]Chapman, *Cancels* (London: Constable & Co., 1930), p. 55.

POEMS, | SUPPOSED TO HAVE BEEN WRITTEN AT BRISTOL, | BY THOMAS ROWLEY,
AND OTHERS, | IN THE FIFTEENTH CENTURY; | THE GREATEST PART NOW FIRST
PUBLISHED FROM THE MOST | AUTHENTIC COPIES, WITH AN ENGRAVED SPECIMEN |
OF ONE OF THE MSS. | TO WHICH ARE ADDED, | A PREFACE, | AN INTRODUCTORY
ACCOUNT OF THE | SEVERAL PIECES, | AND | A GLOSSARY. | LONDON: | Printed
for T. PAYNE and SON, | at the MEWS-GATE. | [*single rule*] | M DCC LXXVII.

*Collation:*    $8^{o}$.   [a]$^2$ b$^8$ c$^4$ (±c4) B-U$^8$ X$^2$ [\$4 (-a1, a2, c3, X2) signed],
168 leaves, pp. *i-ii* iii-xiii *xiv* xv-xxv *xxvi* xxvii *xxviii*, 1-63 *64-66*
67-172 *173-74* 175-308 [misnumbering xiii as xii, misprinting 206 as 06]

*Contents:*   a1$^a$: title (verso blank); a2$^a$: 'THE | CONTENTS | OF THIS VOLUME.';
b1$^a$: 'PREFACE.'; b5$^b$ blank; b6$^a$: 'INTRODUCTORY ACCOUNT | OF THE | SEVERAL
PIECES | CONTAINED IN THIS VOLUME.'; c3$^b$ blank; c4$^a$: 'ADVERTISEMENT. |
*THE Reader is defired to obferve, | that the notes at the bottom of the |
feveral pages, throughout the following | part of this book, are all co
pied from | MSS. in the hand-writing of* Thomas | Chatterton.'; c4$^b$ blank;
B1$^a$: 'ECLOGUE THE FIRST.'; B3$^b$: 'ECLOGUE THE SECOND.'; B6$^b$: 'ECLOGUE THE
THIRD.'; C2$^a$: 'ELINOURE AND JUGA.'; C4$^a$: 'TO JOHNE LADGATE.'; C4$^a$: 'SONGE
TO AELLA, LORDE OF THE CASTLE OF | BRYSTOWE YNNE DAIES OF YORE.'; C5$^b$:
'The underwritten Lines were compofed by JOHN | LADGATE, a Prieft in Lon
don, and fent to | ROWLIE, as an Anfwer to the preceding *Songe | of AE
lla.*'; C6$^b$: 'THE TOURNAMENT. | AN INTERLUDE.'; D6$^b$: 'BRISTOWE TRAGEDIE:
OR THE DETHE OF | SYR CHARLES BAWDIN.'; E8$^b$ blank; F1$^a$: 'AELLA: | A | TRA
GYCAL ENTERLUDE, | OR | DISCOORSEYNGE TRAGEDIE, | WROTENN BIE | THOMAS
ROWLEIE; | PLAIEDD BEFORE | MASTRE CANYNGE, ATTE HYS HOWSE NEMPTE | THE
RODDE LODGE; | [ALSOE BEFORE THE DUKE OF NORFOLCK, JOHAN | HOWARD.]'; F1$^b$:
'PRESONNES REPRESENTEDD.'; F2$^a$: 'EPISTLE TO MASTRE CANYNGE ON | AELLA.';
F4$^a$: 'LETTER TO THE DYGNE MASTRE | CANYNGE.'; F6$^a$: 'ENTRODUCTIONNE.'; F6$^b$:
'AELLA.'; M7$^a$: 'GODDWYN; A TRAGEDIE. | BY THOMAS ROWLEIE.'; O6$^a$: 'AN EX
CELENTE BALADE | OF CHARITIE: | As wroten bie the gode Priefte THOMAS ROW
LEY,   1464.'; P1$^b$: 'BATTLE OF HASTINGS.'; T2$^a$: 'ONN OURE LADIES CHYRCHE.';
T3$^b$: 'THE STORIE OF WILLIAM CANYNGE.'; T7$^b$: 'ON HAPPIENESSE, by WILLIAM
CANYNGE.'; T8$^a$: 'THE GOULER"S REQUIEM, by the fame.'; T8$^b$: 'THE ACCOUNTE
OF W. CANYNGES | FEAST.'; U1$^a$: 'A GLOSSARY OF UNCOMMON WORDS | IN THIS VOL
UME.'; U1$^b$: 'EXPLANATION OF THE LETTERS OF | REFERENCE.'; U2$^a$: 'A GLOSS
ARY.'; X2$^a$: 'ERRATA.'; X2$^b$ blank.

HT]   POEMS, &c.    B1$^a$

# P O E M S,

SUPPOSED TO HAVE BEEN WRITTEN AT BRISTOL,

## BY THOMAS ROWLEY, AND OTHERS,

IN THE FIFTEENTH CENTURY;

THE GREATEST PART NOW FIRST PUBLISHED FROM THE MOST
AUTHENTIC COPIES, WITH AN ENGRAVED SPECIMEN
OF ONE OF THE MSS.

TO WHICH ARE ADDED,

## A   P R E F A C E,

AN INTRODUCTORY ACCOUNT OF THE
SEVERAL PIECES,

AND

## A   G L O S S A R Y.

L O N D O N:

Printed  for  T.  P A Y N E  and  S O N,
at  the  M E W S - G A T E.

MDCCLXXVII.

---

Fig. II.  Title page of Tyrwhitt's first edition of *Rowley Poems*

$\overset{\frown}{\text{AELLA.}}$   F6$^b$

GODDWYN; A <u>TRAGEDIE</u>.   M8$^b$

RT] according to title of poem

ELINOURE AND JUGA.   [C3$^a$ *no stop*]

THE TOURNAMENT.   [C7$^a$ *no stop*]

ENGLYSH METAMORPHOSIS: | BOOKE Ist.   [Q3$^b$ *no stop*]

BATTLE OF HASTINGS.   [R4$^b$ *no stop*]

CW]   C8$^b$ The [Styll,]   D5$^b$ Soe [Soe,]   E2$^a$ I make ["I make]   G2$^a$
MANNE. [MANNE,]   G2$^b$ Droried [Drooried]   G5$^a$ SECOND [SECONDE]
G8$^b$ $\overset{\frown}{\text{AELLA}}$: [AELLA.]   M1$^a$ $\overset{\frown}{\text{AELLA}}$. [AELLA,]

*Typography:*   21 ll. (b1$^b$), 136(156) x 92mm., 120R.; verse measure, 90mm.
(Q5$^a$); advertisement and glossary introduction in italics; glossary in
double columns.

*Press figures:*   2: P5$^b$
             4: E7$^b$
             7: L6$^a$, Q7$^a$

*Plates:*   Facing T8$^b$: 'The Accounte of W. Canynges Feast'; upper right corner:
'*to face page 288.*'; lower left corner: '*I. Strutt, Sculpt.*' (119 x 93mm.)

*Notes:*   1. Ink mark on title (resembling a square bracket: ]) after 'SON,':
*M* (YP.C39.1777) and *O*$^1$ (XL 25.26 [Poe] 28645 1777).
2. MSS. notes by John Fry: *B* (B.5194); William Hale's copies of George
Catcott's transcripts of Chatterton's originals: *B* (B.18996); MSS. notes
by E. H. W. Meyerstein: *L* (CUP.401.g.20).

*Reviewed:*   *BMD*, 1 (1777), 114*ff.*; *CR*, 43 (Feb. 1777), 81–89; *G*, No. 14964
(Feb. 1777), 1; *GM*, 47 (May 1777), 205–08; (June 1777), 275–79; (July
1777), 305–07 and 317; (Aug. 1777), 361–65; (Sept. 1777), 413–14 and
425–27; (Oct. 1777), 481–82; (Nov. 1777), 529; 48 (July 1778), 347–48;
(Aug. 1778), 403; *MR*, ser. 1, 56 (Apr. 1777), 256–65; (May 1777), 321–
28; (June 1777), 445–49; *NB*, pt. 2 (1777), 344.

*Copies examined:*   *L* (C.39.f.1; CUP.401.g.20; 685.g.23; C.39.f.18); *O* (2799.
e.288; Vet. A5.e.2122); *O* (XL 25.26 [Poe] 28645 1777); *B* (B.5194; B.
18996); *M* (YP.C39.1777); *LD* (facsimile reprint by the Scolar Press,
Menston, England, 1969, of a copy in the Leeds University Library).

## 3. Rowley Poems (London: T. Payne, 1777; 2nd. edn.)

POEMS, [&c. as before except: . . . THE GREATEST PART NOW FIRST PUBLISH
ED | FROM THE MOST AUTHENTIC COPIES, | WITH AN ENGRAVED SPECIMEN OF ONE
OF THE MSS. | TO WHICH ARE ADDED, | A PREFACE, | AN INTRODUCTORY ACCOUNT |
OF THE SEVERAL PIECES, | AND | A GLOSSARY. | THE SECOND EDITION. | LON
DON: . . .] M DCC LXXVII.

*Collation:* $8^o$. [a]$^2$ b$^8$ c$^4$ B–U$^8$ X$^2$ [$4 (–a1, a2, c3, X2) signed], 168 lea-
ves, pp. *i–ii* iii–xiii *xiv* xv–xxv *xxvi* xxvii *xxviii*, 1–63 *64–66* 67–172
*173–74* 175–308 [misprinting 202 as 02, misnumbering 246 as 249, unnumbered: 297]

Contents &c. as before.

RT] according to title of poem
THE DETHE OF | SYR CHARLES BAWDIN. [E4$^a$ SIR]
AELLA: | A TRAGYCAL ENTERLUDE. [G8$^b$ AELLA.]
ENGLYSH METAMORPHOSIS, &c. [O5$^b$ &c. *omitted*]
BATTLE OF HASTINGS. [P4$^b$ *no stop*]

CW] C6$^a$ EHE [THE] C8$^b$ The [Styll,] D5$^b$ Soe [Soe,] E1$^b$ "Howe ["How]
E2$^a$ I make ["I make] G2$^b$ Droried [Drooried] G8$^b$ AELLA: [AELLA.]
M1$^a$ AELLA. [AELLA,] M1$^b$ EGWINA [EGWINA.] M2$^b$ EDWINA, [EGWINA.]
M4$^a$ Botte [Botte,] O4$^b$ Stept [Stepte] X1$^a$ Wayne [Wayne,] X1$^b$
ERRA- [*The*]

Typography &c. as before.

Press figures as before.

Plates &c. as before.

*Notes:* 1. Pleased with the favourable reception awarded the first edition,
Tyrwhitt wrote to George Catcott on 13 March 1777: 'Mr. Payne has begun
to print a second Edition of the Poems, which is intended to be merely
a Copy of the first, as it is thought that the little Additions or im-
provements, which might be made, would not justify the injury which the
Purchasers of the former Edition would suffer by having the value of
their Books diminished.' (Quoted from *RES*, 7 (July 1931), 325). The errata of the first edition are corrected in this one, but there are no
other verbal changes. The type fount is somewhat larger throughout, especially in the Preface.

2. MSS. notes by George Symes Catcott: *O* (Don.e.597); signature of J.
Addington Symonds: *L* (11643.cc.2).
*Copies examined:* *L* (11643.cc.2; C.39.f.2); *O* (Don.e.597; 12 ⊖ 1952).


## 4. ROWLEY POEMS (LONDON: T. PAYNE, 1778; 3RD. EDN.)


*Half-title:* POEMS, | SUPPOSED TO HAVE BEEN WRITTEN AT BRISTOL, | BY THOMAS
ROWLEY, AND OTHERS, | IN THE FIFTEENTH CENTURY.

*Title:* POEMS, | SUPPOSED TO HAVE BEEN WRITTEN AT BRISTOL, | BY THOMAS ROW
LEY, AND OTHERS, | IN THE FIFTEENTH CENTURY. | THE THIRD EDITION; | TO
WHICH IS ADDED | AN APPENDIX, | CONTAINING SOME OBSERVATIONS UPON THE |
LANGUAGE OF THESE POEMS; | TENDING TO PROVE, | THAT THEY WERE WRITTEN,
NOT BY ANY ANCIENT | AUTHOR, | BUT ENTIRELY BY THOMAS CHATTERTON. | LON
DON: | Printed for T. PAYNE and SON, | at the MEWS-GATE. | [*single
rule*] | M DCC LXXVIII.

*Collation:* 8°. [a]³ b⁸ c⁴ B–U⁸ X² Y⁸ Z⁵ [$4 (–a1, a2, a3, c3, c4, X2, Z3,
Z4) signed], 183 leaves, pp. [2] *i–ii* iii–xxv *xxvi* xxvii *xxviii*, 1–63
*64–66* 67–172 *173–74* 175–307 *308–10* 311–33 *334* [misnumbering 246 as 249,
unnumbered: 297]

*Contents:* a1ᵃ: half-title (verso blank); a2ᵃ: title (verso blank); a3ᵃ:
'THE | CONTENTS | OF THIS VOLUME.'; b1ᵃ &c. as before; Y1ᵃ: 'APPENDIX; |
CONTAINING | SOME OBSERVATIONS UPON THE | LANGUAGE OF THE POEMS | AT
TRIBUTED TO ROWLEY; | TENDING TO PROVE, | THAT THEY WERE WRITTEN, NOT BY |
ANY ANCIENT AUTHOR, BUT ENTIRELY | BY THOMAS CHATTERTON. | Tum levis haud
ultra latebras jam quaerit imago, | Sed sublime volans nocti fe immifcuit
atrae. | VIRGIL, AE. X.' (verso blank); Y2ᵃ: 'APPENDIX, &c.'; Z5ᵇ blank.

HT] as before, *plus* APPENDIX, &c.   Y2ᵃ

RT] according to title of poem
THE DETHE OF | SYR CHARLES BAWDIN.   [E4ᵃ SIR]
AELLA: | A TRAGYCAL ENTERLUDE.   [G8ᵇ AELLA.]
BATTLE OF HASTINGS.   [P4ᵇ *no stop*]

CW] b4ᵃ ing,   [ing; ]; *remainder as in 2nd. edn., except* M4ᵃ Botte [Botte,] *is here corrected.*

Typography &c. as before.

*Press figures:*    1:    G7$^a$, H7$^b$, I7$^b$, M2$^b$, N5$^b$, P7$^b$, R5$^a$, U7$^b$

2:    I4$^b$, L5$^a$, Q8$^a$, R3$^b$, S4$^b$, T6$^b$

3:    b4$^b$, c2$^b$, c4$^b$, G1$^b$, K5$^a$, S3$^b$

4:    B5$^a$, U7$^a$

5:    E7$^b$, F8$^b$, K7$^b$, M3$^b$, P2$^b$, T3$^b$, Y6$^b$

6:    D5$^b$, E2$^b$, F7$^b$, H4$^b$, O8$^b$

7:    D8$^b$, N2$^b$, O8$^a$, Q2$^b$

Plates &c. as before.

*Notes:*    1. This edition is basically a reprint of its two predecessors, with one important addition. In accordance with his opinion that the most reliable way of determining the authenticity of the Poems was to examine thoroughly all the available evidence, Tyrwhitt added at the end of this third edition the controversial 'Appendix' in which, after careful consideration, he concluded that the Poems' author was Thomas Chatterton. For the benefit of those who had already purchased the first or second edition, the 'Appendix', which continues the signing and pagination of those editions, was published separately, price 6d.

2. This edition was subsequently reprinted, with minor alterations and an introduction by Maurice Evan Hare, Oxford at the Clarendon Press, 1911.

*Reviewed:*    BMD, 3 (1778), 309ff.; MR (Monthly Catalogue Poetical), 58 (June 1778), p. 472.

*Copies examined:*    L (C.39.f.3; 1162.k.5); O (Douce C.244); O[1] (XL 25.26 [Poe] 1778).

The *Miscellanies* was edited by John Broughton who referred to himself as 'one who had a slight knowledge of [Chatterton] in his life time, but not enough to be acquainted with his merits, until too late . . .; [I have] employed a few leisure hours in collecting the following miscellany.' (pp. xxii-xxiii). Broughton's competence as a reliable editor has been questioned recently by D. S. Taylor, who writes that in a letter dated 6 May 1770, 'Chatterton, through Cary [the poet's closest friend], instructs Broughton and twelve other acquaintances to search the *Freeholder's Magazine* for his efforts. The assumption has been, apparently, that this association with Chatterton enabled Broughton to make . . . attributions with authority.'[1]

Broughton's claim, that the pieces in the *Miscellanies* are 'genuine and acknowledged productions of Thomas Chatterton', is investigated by Taylor and he observes that of the forty-three entries in that collection, twenty-three were published either anonymously or pseudonymously in periodicals prior to Chatterton's departure to London on 24 April 1770. Only one of those pieces is unsupported by evidence of authenticity. Of the remaining twenty works published after 24 April, two were taken from periodicals dated after the poet's death where they are specifically connected with Chatterton. A third piece, published in the *Town and Country Magazine* for September 1770 and signed 'D. B.', is so obviously the work of Chatterton that the attribution is secure.

There remain seventeen works of doubtful authenticity. Taylor postulates that Broughton, in collaboration with Cary (who wrote the 'Elegy to the Memory of Mr. Thomas Chatterton', p. 241), and others chose these anonymous contributions to various periodicals, basing their selection on three brief passages from Chatterton's letters of July 1770. In those letters Chatterton claimed to have published extensively in a number of magazines and on an amusing balance sheet on Mayor William Beckford's death wrote of having made money from publishing some elegies. Taylor maintains there is 'enough evidence in addition to the 1778 attribution to give eleven of them to

[1]Taylor, 'The Authenticity of Chatterton's *Miscellanies in Prose and Verse*', *Papers of the Bibliographical Society of America*, 60 (1961), p. 289.

Chatterton beyond a doubt . . . but the remaining nine attributions have no solid evidential support.'[2] Those nine are 'Elegy on W. Beckford, Esq.' (p. 76), 'The Prophecy' (p. 105), 'Anecdote of Judge Jeffries' (p. 138), 'On the Origin and Design of Sculpture' (p. 142), 'The Adventures of a Star' (p. 149), 'Tony Selwood's Description of a Modern Antique Character' (p. 209), 'The Hunter of Oddities, No. 1' (p. 214), 'The Hunter of Oddities, No. 3' (p. 221) and 'Anecdote of Lord C---d' (p. 234).

The edition was published at the price of 3s. 6d. sewed, by Fielding and Walker, Paternoster Row. It has no independent textual authority having been derived entirely from previously printed sources.

[2]Taylor, *ibid.*

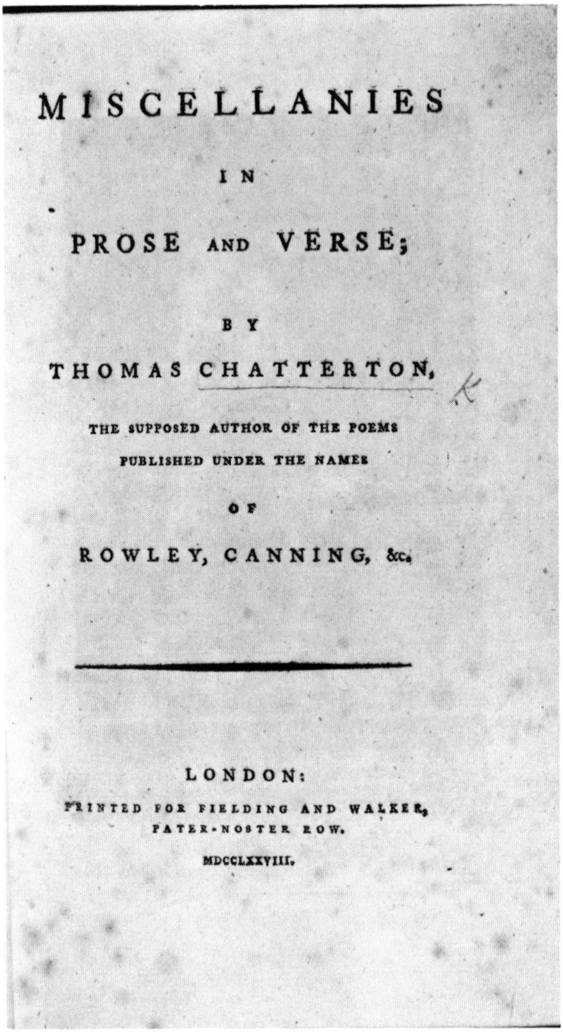

# MISCELLANIES

## I N

## PROSE AND VERSE;

B Y

## THOMAS CHATTERTON,

THE SUPPOSED AUTHOR OF THE POEMS

PUBLISHED UNDER THE NAMES

O F

## ROWLEY, CANNING, &c.

LONDON:

PRINTED FOR FIELDING AND WALKER,
PATER-NOSTER ROW.

MDCCLXXVIII.

Fig. III. Title page of *Miscellanies in Prose and Verse*, 1778

*alf-title:*   MISCELLANIES | IN | PROSE AND VERSE; | BY | THOMAS CHATTERTON.

*itle:*   MISCELLANIES | IN | PROSE AND VERSE; | BY | THOMAS CHATTERTON, | THE
SUPPOSED AUTHOR OF THE POEMS | PUBLISHED UNDER THE NAMES | OF | ROWLEY,
CANNING, &c. | [*single rule*] | LONDON: | PRINTED FOR FIELDING AND WALKER, |
PATER-NOSTER ROW. | MDCCLXXVIII.

*ollation:*   8$^O$. a-b$^8$ B-Q$^8$ R$^4$ [$4 (-a1, a2, R3, R4) signed)], 140 leaves,
pp. *i-iv* v-vii *viii* ix-xxxii, 1-248 [ misnumbering 207 as 107 ]

*ontents:*   a1$^a$: half-title (verso blank); a2$^a$: title (verso blank); a3$^a$:
'CONTENTS.'; a4$^b$ blank; a5$^a$: 'PREFACE.'; b4$^b$: '*To the Printer of the St.
James's Chronicle.*'; B1$^a$: text; R1$^a$: 'ELEGY, | TO THE MEMORY | OF MR.
THOMAS CHATTERTON, | LATE OF BRISTOL.'; R3$^b$ blank; R4$^a$: 'BOOKS printed
for FIELDING and WALKER.'

[T]   MISCELLANIES.   B1$^a$

[T]   according to title of piece
PREFACE.   [b2$^a$ PREFACE, ]
GODRED CROVAN.   [D1$^a$, D3$^a$ *no stop*]
THE CONSULIAD.   [H3$^a$ *no stop*]
MEMOIRS OF | SIR WILLIAM CANYNGE.   [I6$^a$, I7$^a$, I8$^a$ CANNINGE. ]
A HUNTER OF ODDITIES.   [P8$^a$ *no stop*]
THE UNFORTUNATE FATHERS.   [Q8$^b$ *no stop*]

[W]   b6$^a$ My [Mie]  B7$^b$ GOD- [CERDICK, ]  C4$^a$ Madded ["Madded]  C4$^b$ "Sel
wyn ["Selwyn, ]  F1$^a$, F6$^a$ ELEGY [ELEGY, ]  G4$^b$ Accept [Accept, ]  G7$^a$
Monarchs! ["Monarchs!"]  H6$^b$ XII. When, [XII. When]  I1$^b$ from [fromm]
I8$^b$ ANTIQIUITY [ANTIQUITY]  K3$^a$ *no catchword* [To]  K7$^a$ *no catchword*
[ON]  L5$^b$ qusition [quisition]  N1$^a$ romantic [romantic. ]  P4$^b$ *no
catchword* [NUMBER]  P8$^a$ the [in]  Q8$^b$ ELEGY [ELEGY, ]

*ypography:*   26 ll. (I5$^a$), 144(155) x 83mm., 112R.; verse measure, 85mm. (H1$^b$);
in prose and verse, not divided.

*ress figures:*   1:  a8$^a$, C5$^a$, E7$^a$, F5$^b$, G6$^b$, H5$^b$, I7$^b$, K2$^b$, L8$^b$, M5$^b$, N7$^b$,
          O1$^b$, P1$^b$, R2$^b$
      2:  a5$^a$, b3$^b$, M5$^a$, N7$^b$
      3:  b7$^a$, B8$^a$, D4$^b$, E5$^b$, F6$^b$, I4$^b$, K8$^a$, L5$^b$, Q2$^b$

*lates:*   Facing K3$^b$: '*Saxon Achievements. Page 134.*'; six inverted triangu-
lar shields and the front and back of two amulets, all delineated by
Chatterton. (165 x 107mm.)

*otes:*   1. MSS. notes by Thomas De Quincey and others thought to be by Samuel Taylor Coleridge: *B* (B.20675).

*Reviewed:*   BMD, 4 (1779), p. 266ff. and 369-74; *GM*, 48 (Sept. 1778), p. 424;
   *MR* (Monthly Catalogue), 59, art. 47 (Nov. 1778), p. 395.
*Copies examined:*   L (C.39.f.4); B (B.20675); BPL (facsimile reprint by Gregg
   International Publishers Ltd., Farnborough, England, 1971, of a copy in
   the Brighton Public Library).


## 6. CROFT, LOVE AND MADNESS (LONDON: G. KEARSLY, 1780)


LOVE and MADNESS. | *A STORY TOO TRUE.* | In a SERIES of LETTERS between
Parties, whofe | Names would perhaps be mentioned, were | they lefs
known, or lefs lamented. | [*single rule*] | *Governor.* Who did the bloody
deed? | *Oroonoko.* The deed was mine. | Bloody I know it is, and I expect |
Your laws fhould tell me fo. Thus, felf-condemned, | I do refign myfelf
into your hands, | The hands of Juftice. | OROONOKO. | [*single rule*] |
LONDON: | Printed for G. KEARSLY, at No. 46, near | Serjeants Inn, Fleet
Street. | M,DCC,LXXX.

*Collation:*   $8^O$. in 4s [A]$^4$ B-2P$^4$, 152 leaves, pp. *i-iii* iv-vi *vii-viii*, 1-
   296.

*Selections of Chatterton:*   Letter XLIX: R3$^a$- 2I2$^b$ (pp. 125-244).

*Typography:*   27 (28) ll. (Q2$^a$), 140(152) x 84mm., 102R.; some italics throughout; in prose and verse; 2H2$^a$-2H4$^a$ in double columns.

*Notes:*   1. *Love and Madness* is a collection of letters purporting to be the
   correspondence between the Reverend William Hackman and his murder victim,
   Martha Ray; in fact, the letters were written by Sir Herbert Croft. Having obtained from Chatterton's family a number of the boy's hitherto unpublished holograph letters and poems, Croft seized the opportunity to
   include the pieces, without the permission of the poet's mother or sister,
   among his fabricated collection of Hackman-Ray letters. The poems include
   'Apostate Will', 'The Resignation' and 'Happiness', and there are eight of
   Chatterton's London letters. The book was many times reprinted.

*Reviewed:*   CR, 53 (June 1782), p. 421.

*Copies examined:*   L (G.14309; 12651.ff.21).

# 7. ROWLEY POEMS (LONDON: T. PAYNE & SON, 1782)

This edition of the Rowley Poems, price £1 1s, was intended to re-
fute the evidence in Tyrwhitt's 'Appendix' to the third edition (1778) that
the Poems had been forged and to prove that the author of them was, in fact,
the fifteenth century priest that Chatterton claimed he was. The edition,
though dated 1782, was actually published by Thomas Payne before Christmas
Day, 1781. In a letter dated 25 December 1781, George Steevens wrote to
the Reverend William Cole that 'neither Bryant nor Milles will gain additional credit by their respective works . . . Tyrwhitt is preparing to answer
them both'.[1] That answer came in the *Vindication of the Appendix* (1782).
On 21 January 1782 Steevens again wrote to Cole: 'You know, I imagine, that
Tyrwhitt, Tom Warton, Mr. Malone, and others have taken up their pens in
opposition to the books of Bryant and Milles. My friend, Dr. Johnson says,
he is sorry for the former, who possesses a very great and deserved reputation; as to the Dean's performance, it is everywhere treated as it de-
serves, and to its fate he resigns it without concern.'[2]

Milles' edition added fuel to the already heated debate about the Poems'
authenticity and in rebuttal there appeared in quick succession the follow-
ing: *The Prophecy of Queen Emma*, edited by W. J. Mickle; Edmond Malone's
*Cursory Observations on the Poems Attributed to Thomas Rowley*; *An Enquiry
into the Authenticity of the Poems Attributed to Thomas Rowley*, by Thomas
Warton; the anonymous *Archaeological Epistle to the Rev. and Worshipful
Jeremiah Milles*, attributed to William Mason; and the anonymous pamphlet,
*An Examination of the Poems Attributed to Thomas Rowley and William Canynge*.
All were published in 1782.

[1] *L* (Add. MS. 5852, f. 66).
[2] *L* (Add. MS. 6401, f. 170).

POEMS, | SUPPOSED TO HAVE BEEN WRITTEN AT BRISTOL, | IN THE FIFTEENTH
CENTURY, | By THOMAS ROWLEY, PRIEST, &c. | WITH A | COMMENTARY, | IN
WHICH | THE ANTIQUITY OF THEM IS CONSIDERED, | AND DEFENDED. | BY JER
EMIAH MILLES, D. D. | DEAN OF EXETER. | [*single rule*] | *RENASCENTUR QUAE*
*JAM CECIDERE.* | HOR. DE ARTE POETICA. | [*double rule*] | *LONDON:* | PRINT
ED FOR T. PAYNE, AND SON, AT THE MEWS GATE. | M.DCC.LXXXII.

*Collation:* 4°. [a]-b$^4$ c$^2$ B-3Z$^4$ 4A$^1$ 4B$^1$ [$2 (-a1, a2, c2; +3R3) signed],
284 leaves, pp. *i-iii* iv-xx, 1-545 *546-48* [misprinting 75 as 7]

*Contents:* a1$^a$: title (verso blank); a2$^a$: 'ADVERTISEMENT.'; a3$^a$: 'THE | CON
TENTS | OF THIS VOLUME.'; a4$^a$: 'PREFACE | TO THE FORMER EDITIONS.'; b2$^b$:
'INTRODUCTORY ACCOUNT | OF THE | SEVERAL PIECES CONTAINED IN THIS VOL
UME.'; c2$^b$: 'NOTE OF REFERENCE | TO THE | FOLLOWING SHEETS.'; B1$^a$: 'PRE
LIMINARY | DISSERTATION.'; F1$^a$: text; 3M3$^a$: 'POSTSCRIPT.'; 3X2$^a$: 'A GLOS
SARY OF UNCOMMON WORDS | IN THIS VOLUME.'; 3X2$^b$: 'EXPLANATION OF THE LET
TERS | OF REFERENCE.'; 3X3$^a$: 'A GLOSSARY.'; 4A1$^a$: 'ERRATA.'; 4B1$^a$: 'AD
DITION TO PAGE 191.' (verso blank).

HT] GODDWYN; A TRAGEDIE. 2O3$^a$
   POEMS, &c. 3D4$^a$

RT] according to title of poem
   N$^o$. 2. [Q1$^a$ N$^o$. I.]
   THE BRISTOWE TRAGEDIE. [2X1$^a$*no stop*]

CW] G2$^b$ "The [The] R4$^b$ That [That,] Z4$^b$ Chatterton, [Chatterton;]
   2C2$^a$ ELLA. [CELMONDE,] 2Q1$^a$ *no footnote catchword* [This] 2Q4$^b$
   distinguish [guish] 3B3$^b$ THE [SONGE] 3G2$^a$ Believe [Beleive]

*Typography:* 34 ll. (E3$^b$), 184(200) x 124mm., 154R.; verse measure, 110mm.
   (3A1$^a$); advertisement in italics; glossary in double columns.

*Press figures:* 1: S1$^b$, 2N2$^b$, 2Q4$^b$, 2Z4$^b$, 3X4$^a$, 3Y3$^b$
   2: a4$^b$, D1$^b$, E3$^b$, F1$^b$, L4$^b$, 2F4$^a$, 2S3$^b$, 2U3$^b$, 2Z3$^b$, 3A4$^b$,
      3C2$^b$, 3S1$^b$, 3T3$^b$, 3U2$^b$, 3Z1$^b$
   3: a4$^a$, b2$^b$, G1$^b$, H2$^b$, I4$^a$, M3$^b$, U4$^a$, X4$^a$, 2B1$^b$, 2E3$^b$,
      2P3$^a$, 3B2$^b$, 3C1$^b$, 3D3$^a$, 3L4$^a$
   5: B3$^b$, C1$^b$, K4$^a$, Y1$^b$, 2G3$^b$, 2O1$^b$, 2Q3$^b$, 2R3$^b$, 2T2$^b$, 2X1$^b$,
      2Y3$^b$, 3B4$^a$, 3E3$^b$, 3F3$^b$, 3L2$^b$, 3P4$^a$, 3R3$^b$, 3Y4$^b$, 3Z2$^b$
   6: 3Q4$^b$, 3S2$^b$
   7: O4$^b$, Z1$^b$, 2H1$^b$, 2I1$^a$, 2K3$^a$, 2M4$^a$, 3I2$^b$, 3M4$^b$
   9: 2A2$^b$, 2I1$^b$, 2M3$^a$, 2R2$^b$, 2X2$^b$, 3A1$^b$, 3H4$^b$, 3I4$^a$, 3K3$^b$,

# P O E M S,

SUPPOSED TO HAVE BEEN WRITTEN AT BRISTOL,

IN THE FIFTEENTH CENTURY.

By THOMAS ROWLEY, PRIEST, &c.

WITH A

C O M M E N T A R Y,

IN WHICH

THE ANTIQUITY OF THEM IS CONSIDERED,

AND DEFENDED.

BY JEREMIAH MILLES, D. D.

DEAN OF EXETER.

*RENASCENTUR QUÆ JAM CECIDERE.*
HOR. DE ARTE POETICA.

*L O N D O N:*

PRINTED FOR T. PAYNE, AND SON, AT THE MEWS GATE.

M. DCC. LXXXII,

IV. Title page of Milles' edition of *Rowley Poems*, 1782

$3M3^b$, $3O1^b$, $3R4^b$, $3U3^b$

10: $P3^b$, $Q3^b$, $R3^b$, $T1^b$, $2D1^b$, $2T1^b$, $3G3^b$, $3K3^a$, $3N4^a$, $3R1^a$

*Plates:* Facing $3M2^b$: 'The Accounte of W. Canynges Feast'; upper right corner: '*to face P. 452*'; lower left corner: '*I. Strutt Sculp*$^t$.' (138 x 110mm.).

*Notes:* 1) This edition is almost entirely a reprint of Tyrwhitt's first edition; it is almost void of textual interest, but it does contain the following additions:

   i) 'Songe of Seyncte Baldwyne' and 'Songe of Seyncte Warburghe' (p. 433), printed from a George Catcott transcript.

   ii) lines 1-63 of 'The Merrie Tricks of Laymyngetowne' (p.183), from the holograph British Library Add. MS. 24891, f.5.

   iii) lines 81-90 of 'Amphitryon. A Burletta.' (p. 521), quoted from a now lost manuscript given to Milles by John Rudhall and said to be in Chatterton's hand.

   iv) the prose account of Lamington from 'Emendals' found in 'A Discourse on Brystowe' (p. 180).

   v) lines 177-96, 249-58 of 'The Parlyamente of Sprytes' (pp. 185, 189).

   vi) the description of William Canynge in 'Abstracts from Letters' (p. 444n).

2) MSS. notes by John Sherwen: *L* (C.39.h.19, C.39.h.18); MSS. notes by Horace Walpole: *L* (C.39.i.19); collection of Chattertoniana donated by John Haslewood: *L* (C.39.h.20); Chatterton's signature on a small piece of paper and anonymous MSS. notes: *B* (B.11189).

3) Numerical catchwords in footnotes discontinued after $G4^b$, except on $Q2^a$, where catchword is 'v. 561').

*Reviewed:* *CR*, 53 (June 1782), pp. 401-17; 54 (July 1782), pp. 1-18; *GM*, 51 (Dec. 1781), pp. 555-59; (Suppl. 1781), pp. 609-15, 622-23; 52 (Jan. 1782), pp. 14-15, 27-28; (Feb. 1782), p.76; (Mar. 1782), pp. 107-09, 128-30; (Apr. 1782), pp. 168, 177; (May 1782), pp. 220-21; (Aug. 1782), pp. 379-81; (Sept. 1782), p. 434; *MR*, 66 (Mar. 1782), pp. 206-19; (Apr. 1782), pp. 294-98; (May 1782), pp. 321-34; 67 (Sept. 1782), pp. 161-70; *EM* (Jan. 1782), p. 35.

*Copies examined:* *L* (C.39.h.18; C.39.h.20; C.39.h.19; C.39.i.19; 77.k.11; 641.1.2; 11607.i.19; 11656.r.42); *B* (B.11189).

# 8. Supplement to the Miscellanies (London: T. Becket, 1784)

This *Supplement*, price 2s, was announced as 'in the press' four days (31 July 1778) after the publication of the *Miscellanies*, but did not actually appear until six years later. Apart from the pieces herein included, it has been postulated that lines 1–376 of 'Kew Gardens' were printed off as the first item, then cancelled and later issued as the second *Supplement*, perhaps in 1785[1]; I find no evidence to support this view.

The *Supplement* seems to have been printed almost entirely from manuscripts in Chatterton's hand and is of some textual importance, especially as regards those manuscripts no longer extant. Because George Catcott was specifically connected with almost all the manuscript sources, it may be reasonable to assume that he had a hand in the publication of this *Supplement*.

[1]Meyerstein, p. 325n.

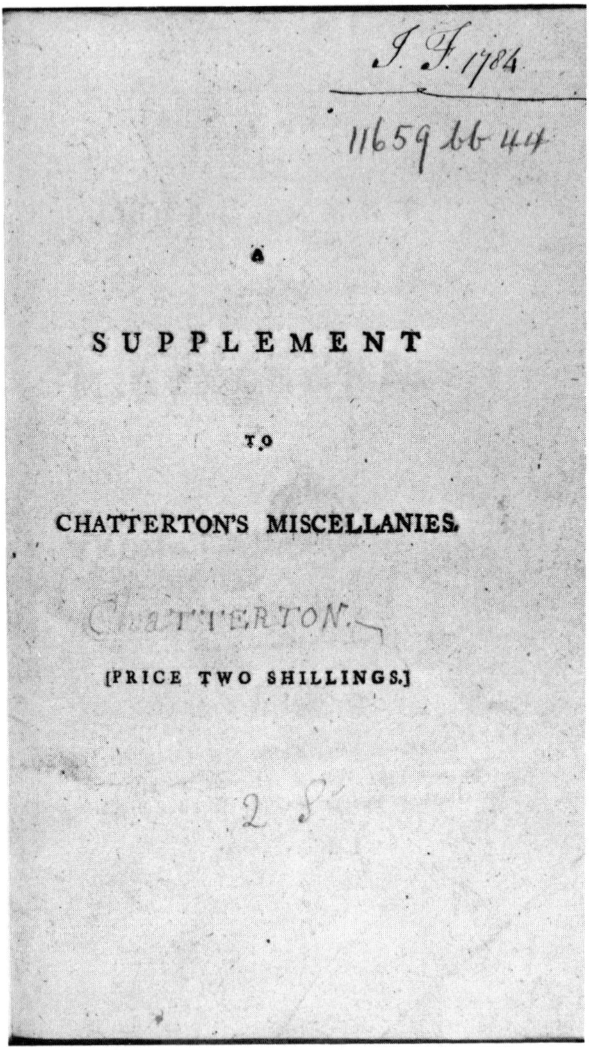

*J. F.* 1784

11659 bb 44

A

# S U P P L E M E N T

T O

## CHATTERTON'S MISCELLANIES.

*Chatterton.*

[PRICE TWO SHILLINGS.]

2 8

Fig. V.   Title page of *Supplement to the Miscellanies*, 1784

*alf-title:*  A | SUPPLEMENT | TO | CHATTERTON'S MISCELLANIES. | [PRICE TWO
SHILLINGS.]

*Title:*  A | SUPPLEMENT | TO THE | MISCELLANIES | OF | THOMAS CHATTERTON. |
[*single rule*] | LONDON: | PRINTED FOR T. BECKET, IN PALL-MALL; | BOOK
SELLER TO HIS ROYAL HIGHNESS THE PRINCE OF | WALES, AND THEIR ROYAL
HIGHNESSES THE PRINCES. | MDCCLXXXIV.

*Collation:*  $8^o$.  [A]$^4$ B-F$^8$ G$^4$  [$4 (-A1, A2, A3, A4, G3, G4) signed]; 48
leaves, pp. [*6*] i-ii, 1-78 *79-80* 81-88.

*Contents:*  A1$^a$: half-title (verso blank); A2$^a$: title (verso blank); A3$^a$:
'ADVERTISEMENT.' (verso blank); A4$^a$: 'CONTENTS.'; B1$^a$: 'TO A FRIEND.';
B2$^a$: 'TO THE | BEAUTEOUS MISS H-L-D.'; B3$^a$: 'ODE | TO | MISS H-L-D.
1768.'; B4$^b$: 'ACROSTIC ON MISS. 1768.'; B5$^a$: 'ACROSTIC ON MISS. 1768.';
B5$^b$: 'TO | MISS H-L-D. 1768.'; B6$^b$: 'TO | MISS H-L-D. 1768.'; B7$^b$: 'TO |
MISS H-L-D. 1768.'; B8$^b$: 'TO | MISS H-L-D. 1768. | WITH A PRESENT.'; C1$^a$:
'TO | MISS H-L-D. 1768.'; C1$^b$: 'TO | MISS C-KE 1768.'; C2$^a$: 'EPISTLE |
TO THE | REVEREND MR. CATCOTT.'; D1$^b$: 'SENTIMENT. 1769.'; D2$^a$: 'THE |
DEFENCE.'; D4$^a$: 'SONG | TO | MR. G. CATCOTT. 1769.'; D5$^b$: 'IN | IMITATION
OF OUR OLD POETS. | ONE CANTO OF AN ANCIENT POEM | CALLED THE | UNKNOWN
KNIGHT OR THE TOURNAMENT:'; E1$^b$: 'IN | IMITATION OF OUR OLD POETS. | ON
OURE LADYES CHIRCH. 1769.'; E3$^a$: 'HECCAR AND GAIRA | AN | AFRICAN ECLOGUE.';
E6$^b$: 'CHATTERTON'S WILL. 1770.'; F4$^b$: 'THE | METHODIST.'; F5$^b$: 'COLIN IN
STRUCTED. 1770.'; F6$^a$: 'A | BURLESQUE CANTATA. 1770.'; F7$^a$: 'SONG. | FANNY
OF THE HILL. 1770.'; F8$^a$: 'BURLETTA. | THE | WOMAN OF SPIRIT. | 1770.';
G1$^a$: 'THE | WOMAN OF SPIRIT.'

[T]  [*double rule*] | SUPPLEMENT | TO | CHATTERTON'S MISCELLANIES. | [*single
rule*]  B1$^a$

[W]  B2$^a$ Rous [Rouse]

*Typography:*  22 ll. (F2$^b$), 144(160) x 83mm., 131R.; verse measure, 82mm. (C5$^b$);
in prose and verse, not divided.

*Reviewed:*  GM, 54 (Nov. 1784), pp. 848-49; MR, 71 (Sept. 1784), p. 229.

*Copies examined:*  L (C.39.f.4; 11659.bb.44; 1162.k.7).

## 9. Supplement to Chatterton's Miscellanies. Kew Gardens. (NP., ND., 1785?)

*No title leaf.*
*Collation:* 8°. B⁸, 8 leaves, pp. 1-16.
*Contents:* B1ᵃ: 'KEW GARDENS.'
HT] SUPPLEMENT | TO | Chatterton's Miscellanies.  B1ᵃ
CW] B5ᵃ *no catchword* [---- happy]
*Typography:* 28 ll. (B7 ), 143(154) x 83mm., 102R., in verse, not divided.
*Notes:* 1) This publication has no independent textual authority, having
been printed from a British Library transcript (first tract in C.39.h.
20) in the supposed handwriting of Isaac Reed. Meyerstein (*Life*, p.
325n) suggests that 'this was probably printed off as the first item
in [the 1784 *Supplement*], and then cancelled; the sig. is B, in fours'.
As Taylor points out (*Works*, 2, p. 1068), however, the type for this
supplement is set up differently from that for 1784. Also, the printing press punch marks in the paper of this work are spaced differently
from those in the 1784 *Supplement*. This publication prints lines 1-
376 of 'Kew Gardens'.


## 10. The Romaunte of a Knyghte  (Rodborough: James Dallaway?, 1788)

THE ROMAVNTE OF A KNYGHTE. (*Decorated below with an engraved floral
design*)
*Collation:* 8°. Single sheet; unsigned, unnumbered.
*Typography:* Verse measure, 161(220) x 110mm.
*Notes:* 1) Published on a single sheet (Rowleyan version only) by James
Dallaway. The one copy examined was removed from opposite p. 522 of
the 1782 edition of the *Rowley Poems*, L (C.39.h.18) where it had been
pasted to the recto of an inter-leaf. At present it constitutes the
84th tract of the British Library's *Fragmenta Antiqua* (CUP.651.e).
*Copies examined:* L (Cup.651.e (84)).

## 11. Barrett, History of Bristol (Bristol: William Pine, 1789)

William Barrett wished to be the first to publish the many Rowleian pieces found in his *History of Bristol*, so consequently, access to the Rowley manuscripts in his possession by the editors of Chatterton prior to 1789 was very much restricted. Here printed for the first time are twelve Rowleian prose works, eight Rowley poems and three of Chatterton's letters. The *History* was used extensively as copy-text for those pieces in many later Chatterton editions, but Barrett's competence as an editor is highly questionable.

The *History* appeared in the summer of 1789; it sold for one guinea and a half to subscribers and two guineas to all other purchasers. The edition was hailed with derision, not only for its many inaccuracies, but also because Barrett insisted on publishing the Chatterton productions under the name of Rowley; this brought down upon him the full vengence of the anti-Rowleians. In vain he endeavoured to stave off the attack by inserting in the *History* engraved facsimiles of the 'antique' manuscripts and feebly he asserted in the preface that whatever judgment might be formed of the writings of Rowley, he had attempted to transcribe them faithfully so that the judicious reader might be better able to form his own opinion concerning the Rowley-Chatterton controversy.

THE | HISTORY | AND | ANTIQUITIES | OF THE | *CITY of BRISTOL;* | COM
PILED FROM | Original RECORDS and authentic MANUSCRIPTS, | In public
Offices or private Hands; | Illuſtrated with COPPER-PLATE PRINTS. |
[*single rule*] | By WILLIAM BARRETT, SURGEON, F. S. A. | [*single rule*] |
[*copper-engraved device*] |[*double rule*] | BRISTOL: | Printed by WIL
LIAM PINE, in Wine-Street; | And fold by G. ROBINSON and Co. *London*;
E. PALMER, J. B. BECKET, T. MILLS, J. NORTON, W. BROWNE, | W. BULGIN,
and J. LLOYD, Bookfellers in *Briſtol*; and by BULL and MEYLER, in *Bath*.

*Collation:*    $4^o$.    [a]$^4$ b$^4$ c$^2$ A-4Q$^4$, 362 leaves, pp. *i-iv* v-xx, 1-704.
     (*Note: There are three extra gatherings signed* 'W', 'WW' *and* 'WWW'
     *respectively*)

*Selections of Chatterton:*    D4$^a$-E1$^b$,  E3$^a$-E4$^a$,  F2$^b$-F3$^a$,  H3$^a$-H3$^b$,  M1$^b$,  2A1$^b$,
     2A2$^a$,  2A2$^a$-2A2$^b$,  2A4$^b$,  2B2$^a$,  2G3$^b$,  3F2$^b$,  3K1$^b$,  3K4$^b$,  3O3$^b$,  3Q1$^b$,  3S2$^b$-
     3S3$^a$,  3U3$^b$,  3Y3$^b$,  3Y4$^b$,  4C4$^b$-4E1$^a$,  4G3$^a$-4G4$^a$,  4G4$^b$-4H1$^b$,  4H2$^b$,  4H3$^a$,
     4H3$^a$-4H4$^a$,  4H4$^a$-4I1$^b$,  4I1$^b$-4I2$^b$,  4I2$^b$-4I3$^a$,  4I4$^a$.

*Plates:*    Facing p. 197: 'BRISTOL CASTLE | *as in 1138*'; folding engraved
     facsimile of drawings by Chatterton; lower left corner: '*T. Rowleie,*
     *Canonicus.* | *delin. 1440*'; lower right corner: '*R. Coffin Sc.*' (321
     x 273mm.).
     Facing p. 636: 'John Chaloner a Monke of Sayncte Augustyne's Mynster';
     engraving of a Rowley manuscript; lower left corner: '*T. Kerrich del.*';
     lower right corner: '*B. Longmate sculp.*' (245 x 206mm.).

*Notes:*    1. *L* (C.60.m.2) is the copy used by Southey and Cottle in the pre-
     paration of their edition of Chatterton's works in 1803; in addition to
     MS. notes in the text, it contains 22 pages of MSS. written by Southey
     and 14 pages in the handwriting of Cottle: the notes consist of ex-
     tracts from Chatterton's own MSS. in the British Library and remarks by
     the editors.
     2. Copper engraved device on title measures 167 x 67mm.

*Reviewed:*    GM, 59 (Oct.1789), pp. 921-24; (Dec. 1789), pp. 1081-85.

*Copies examined:*    L (C.60.m.2); B (B.5325).

THE

# HISTORY

AND

# ANTIQUITIES

OF THE

# *CITY of BRISTOL;*

COMPILED FROM

Original RECORDS and authentic MANUSCRIPTS,

In public Offices or private Hands;

Illuſtrated with **COPPER-PLATE PRINTS.**

By **WILLIAM BARRETT**, SURGEON, F.S.A.

# BRISTOL:

Printed by **WILLIAM PINE**, in Wine-Street;

And ſold by G. ROBINSON and Co. *London*; E. PALMER, J. B. BECKET, T. MILLS, J. NORTON, W. BROWNE,
W. BULGIN, and J. LLOYD, Bookſellers in *Briſtol*; and by BULL and MEYLER, in *Bath*.

Fig. VI.  Title page of Barrett's *History of Bristol*

Fig. VIIa. Engraved title of Sharpe's edition of *Rowley Poems*, 1794

Fig. VIIb. Title page of Sharpe's edition of *Rowley Poems*, 1794

## 2. GREGORY, THE LIFE OF THOMAS CHATTERTON (LONDON: G, KEARSLEY, 1789)

THE | LIFE | OF | THOMAS CHATTERTON, | WITH | CRITICISMS | ON HIS | *GEN
IUS AND WRITINGS,* | AND A CONCISE VIEW | OF THE | CONTROVERSY | CONCERN
ING | *ROWLEY's POEMS.* | [*double rule*] | B̲Y̲ G. GREGORY, DD. F. A. S. |
AUTHOR OF ESSAYS HISTORICAL AND MORAL, &c. | [*single rule*] | Agora com
pobreza aborrecida, | Por hofpicios alheos degradado; | Agora da efper
ança ja adquirida, | De novo mais que nunca derribado. | CAMOENS. |
[*single rule*] | LONDON. | PRINTED FOR G. KEARSLEY, No. 46, FLEET ST
REET. | 1789. | [Price Five Shillings fewed.]

*Collation:*   8°.   [A]³ B–R⁸ S⁴, 135 leaves, pp. *i–iv* v–vi, 1–264.

*Selections of Chatterton:*   Q3$^a$–Q3$^b$: 'The ART of PUFFING, | By a BOOKSELLER'S
JOURNEYMAN.'

*Notes:*   1.   In this biography Gregory publishes from a holograph manuscript
'The Art of Puffing', a Chatterton poem never before printed.

*Copies examined:*   L (276.k.26).

## 3A. ROWLEY POEMS (CAMBRIDGE: L. SHARPE, 1794)

*Engraved title:*   POEMS, | *Supposed to have been written at Bristol in the* 15$^{th}$
*Century.* | *By* T̲H̲O̲M̲A̲S̲ R̲O̲W̲L̲E̲Y̲. | [*engraving*] | *Che trae L'huome del sepol
cro ed in vita il serba. Petrarca.* | *CAMBRIDGE.* | *Printed by B. Flower
for the Editor* | *and sold by J. and J. Merrill & W. H. Lunn, Cambridge,* |
Egertons, Military Library; Debrett, Picadilly, Edwards, Pall Mall, | &
Deighton, Holborn, London.

*Note: Plate mark measures 174 x 113mm.*

*Title:*   POEMS, | SUPPOSED TO HAVE BEEN WRITTEN | AT | BRISTOL, | BY | *THOMAS
ROWLEY, AND OTHERS,* | IN THE FIFTEENTH CENTURY. | [*double rule*] | *CAM
BRIDGE:* | PRINTED BY B. FLOWER, FOR THE EDITOR; | AND SOLD BY THE PRINT
ER; BY J. AND J. MERRILL, | AND W. H. LUNN, CAMBRIDGE; BY THE BOOK- |
SELLERS OF BATH AND BRISTOL; AND BY | EGERTON, MILITARY LIBRARY; ED- |
WARDS, PALL-MALL; DEBRETT, | PICADILLY; AND DEIGHTON, | HOLBORN, LONDON. |

[*double rule*] | 1794.

*Collation:*   8⁰.    [π]² a⁸ b⁷ B–U⁸ X–Y⁴ Z⁵ [$4 (–π1, π2, a4, U4, X3, X4, Y3, Y4, Z3, Z4) signed], 182 leaves, pp. [2] *i–iii* iv–xxx *xxxi–xxxii*, 1–329 *330* [missigning F4 as F3 and N3 as N2; 321 numbered to left rather than to right of running-title]

*Contents:*   π1$^a$: engraved title (verso blank); π2$^a$: title (verso blank); a1$^a$: 'THE | CONTENTS OF THIS VOLUME.'; a2$^a$: 'PREFACE.'; a3$^a$: 'PREFACE | TO THE | FORMER EDITIONS.'; a6$^b$: 'INTRODUCTORY ACCOUNT | OF THE | SEVERAL PIECES | CONTAINED IN THIS VOLUME.'; b3$^b$: 'THE Editor thinks himself happy in the permission of | an ingenious Friend, to insert the follow ing Monody.'; b4$^a$: 'MONODY | ON THE | DEATH OF CHATTERTON.'; b6$^a$: 'AD VERTISEMENT.' (verso blank); b7$^a$: text; U3$^a$: 'A GLOSSARY OF | UNCOMMON WORDS IN THIS VOLUME.'; U3$^b$: 'EXPLANATION | OF THE | LETTERS OF REFER ENCE.'; U4$^b$: 'A GLOSSARY.'; Z5$^b$ blank.

HT]   A͡ELLA.   B5$^b$

   GODDWYN; A TRAGEDIE.   H7$^b$

   POEMS, &c.   O4$^b$

RT]   THE DETHE OF | SYR CHARLES BAWDIN.   [M2$^a$ SIR]

CW]   b3$^a$ MONODY. [MONODY]   B3$^b$ Insteddge [Instedde]   B7$^b$, E2$^a$, F5$^a$, G8$^a$ A͡ELLA. [A͡ELLA,]   F2$^b$ BRISTOWE. [BRYSTOWE.]   G6$^b$ Swifte [The]   I6$^a$ KYNGE. [KYNGE]   K4$^b$ AN [THE]   L4$^a$ Soe [Soe,]   L8$^b$ I make ["I make]   O4$^a$ POEMS [POEMS,]   P4$^a$ I follow [I followe]   P5$^a$ ELINOURE. [ELINOURE]   Q5$^b$ But [Then]   U3$^b$ R. E. [R. C.]   U4$^b$ *Affryghte [*Affryghte.]   U7$^b$ Coupe [Coupe.]   X1$^a$ *Dynneth. [*Dynneth,]   X1$^b$ Encalede. [Encalede,]   Y3$^a$ Morthe, [*Morie,]   Z3$^b$ Unsprytes [Un sprytes,]

*Typography:*   26 ll. (a3$^b$), 158(167) x 82mm., 136R.; verse measure, 76mm. (R1$^a$); in prose and verse, not divided; glossary in double columns.

*Press figures:*   2: a1$^a$

*Plates:*   **Facing** O3$^a$: 'The Accounte of W. Canynges Feast.'; upper right corner: '*to face Page 197*'; lower left corner: '*D. Hood, Sc. Cambridge.*' (172 x 116mm.)

*Notes:*   1. This edition was reprinted from Tyrwhitt's first edition and is prefixed by the anonymous 'Monody on the Death of Chatterton'. An intro ductory note states, 'The Editor thinks himself happy in the permission of an ingenious Friend, to insert the following Monody.' (p. xxiv); the

author of the poem, it was later revealed, was Samuel Taylor Coleridge. An enquiry concerning the identity of the editor of this Cambridge edition was made in *N&Q* (7th ser., 5 (1888), p. 429), with
replies (p. 477) naming him as Lancelot Sharpe who graduated B. A.
from Pembroke College, Cambridge, in 1796 and M. A. in 1800; he died
26 October 1851. New in boards, the edition was priced at 5s.; a
large paper copy, an example of which I have not located, sold for
7s. 6d.

*opies examined:* L(G.18498; C.39.f.10; 1465.d.2); O (280.i.195); O$^1$ (XL 25.
26 [Poe] 1794).


# 3B. Rowley Poems (Cambridge: L. Sharpe, 1799)

*ngraved title:* as **above**

*itle:* POEMS, | SUPPOSED TO | *HAVE BEEN WRITTEN AT BRISTOL,* | IN | The Fif
teenth Century. | [*decorative rule*] | BY | THOMAS ROWLEY, | AND
OTHERS. | [*engraved device*] | [*double rule*] | Cambridge: | PRINTED
FOR THE EDITOR, | SOLD BY MESSRS. MERRIL, AND W. H. LUNN, CAMBRIDGE; |
AND R. B. SCOTT, BRYDGES-STREET, ADJOINING CATHE- | RINE-STREET, STR
AND, LONDON. | 1799.

[*Note: Inscription below engraved device:* 'Che trae l'huome del sep-
olere ed in vita il serba. *Petrarca.*']

*ontents &c.* as above

*ptes:* 1. This is another issue of 13A, with a cancel title-leaf. Apart
from the title, the type-setting is identical to that used in 1794.
This issue is not recorded in any of the Chatterton catalogues or
editions that I have seen and the only copy I have been able to loc-
ate is the one at the Bodleian Library.

2. Watermark on the title leaf is 'B | 1799'.

*ppies examined:* O (Vet. A5.e.2008).

14. ANDERSON, THE WORKS OF THE BRITISH POETS (LONDON: J. AND A. ARCH AND BELL AND BRADFUTE; EDINBURGH: J. MUNDELL, 1794, 95)

*Volume title:* THE | WORKS | OF THE | *BRITISH POETS.* | WITH | PREFACES, | BIOGRAPHICAL AND CRITICAL, | *BY ROBERT ANDERSON, M. D.* | [*double rule*] | *VOLUME ELEVENTH.*

Containing

| | | |
|---|---|---|
| WILKIE, | GLOVER, | JOHNSON, |
| DODSLEY, | SHAW, | WHITEHEAD, (W.) |
| SMART, | LOVIBOND, | JENYNS, |
| LANGHORNE, | PENROSE, | LOGAN, |
| BRUCE, | MICKLE, | WARTON, |
| CHATTERTON, | JAGO, | COTTON, AND |
| GRAEME, | SCOTT, | BLACKLOCK. |

[*double rule*] | LONDON: | PRINTED FOR JOHN & ARTHUR ARCH; AND FOR BELL & BRADFUTE, | AND J. MUNDELL & Cº. EDINBURGH. | [*single rule*] | 1794.

*Title for Chatterton selection:* THE | POETICAL WORKS | OF | THOMAS CHATTERTON.

Containing

| | |
|---|---|
| AELLA, | THE TOURNAMENT, |
| GODDWYN, | ENGLYSH METAMORPHOSIS, |
| BATTLE OF HASTINGS, | ECLOGUES, |
| BALLADE OF CHARITIE, | ELEGIES, |
| ELINOURE AND JUGA, | SONGS, |
| DETHE OF SIR CHARLES BAW- | EPISTLES, |
| DIN, | EPITAPHS, |

&c. &c. &c.

To which is prefixed, | *THE LIFE OF THE AUTHOR.* | [*double rule*] | Behold yon fhade, he bears an antique roll; | With many a 'fcutcheon clad, and many a fcroll; | 'Tis he, the wond'rous youth of *Briftowe's* plain, | That pour'd in *Rowley's* garb his folemn ftrain. | A ftripling fcarcely, and yet more than man, | His race was ended, ere it well began. | Th' indignant fpirit tower'd o'er little men, | He look'd through nature with an angel's ken, | And fcorn'd, with confcious

pride, this petty ſtage, ⌢ | The tardy homage of a thanklefs age. |
The furies wrung his agonizing foul, | And defperation mix'd the Sty
gian bowl. | PRESTON'S EPISTLE TO A YOUNG GENTLEMAN. | [*double rule*] |
EDINBURGH: | PRINTED BY *MUNDELL AND SON*, ROYAL BANK CLOSE. | *Anno.*
1795.

*Collation of volume 11:*    [π]$^1$ $a^8$ $b^4$ A–U$^8$ U$^1$ X–4I$^8$ 4K$^1$, 639 leaves, pp.
[2] *i–v* vi–xxiv, 1–320 + 321–322 + 321–1250.

[*Note: Extra leaf signed 'U' inserted after U8, numbered '321' and
'322'*]

*lections of Chatterton:*   T4$^a$: title to Chatterton selection (verso blank);
T5$^a$: '*THE LIFE OF CHATTERTON.*'; X1$^a$: '*PREFACE,* | TO THE | Firſt Ed
ition, 8vo, 1777, publiſhed by THOMAS TYRWHITT, Efq.'; X1$^b$: 'INTRO
DUCTORY ACCOUNT OF THE SEVERAL PIECES.'; X2$^b$: '*THE WORKS OF CHATTER
TON.*'; 2A3$^a$: '*A GLOSSARY* | OF UNCOMMON WORDS.'; 2A6$^b$: '*MISCELLANIES.*';
2C3$^b$ blank.

*tes:*   1. The poems in this selection are reprinted from Tyrwhitt's first
edition of the *Rowley Poems* (1777), with a number from the *Miscellanies* (1778), and the biographical memoir uses as its sources Croft's
*Love and Madness* (1780) and Gregory's *Life of Chatterton* (1789).
2. The entire text, with the exception of *The Life of Chatterton*, is
printed in double columns.

*pies examined:*    L (11607.ff.1/11).

## 15. The Revenge, a Burletta (London: C. Roworth, 1795)

The composition of *The Revenge*, a Burletta which developed out of the fragmentary *Amphitryon*, came about as the result of an acquaintanceship at the Drury-Lane Theatre between Chatterton and a young man from Cheapside who was part-owner of a music shop. The title page states that the play was acted at Marylebone Gardens in 1770, but no evidence has appeared to support this claim, nor has the music ever been found, except for that to 'The Invitation'.

It was to Mr. Luffman Atterbury that Chatterton sold the copyright for the work, the receipt for the sale of which reads:

> Receiv'd July 6th.; 1770 of Mr. Luffman Atterbury, Five Pounds, Five Shillings, being in full for all the Manuscripts contain'd in this Book, of which I am the Author: for which consideration of Five Pounds, Five Shillings I hereby give up my sole right & property in, and the liberty of printing & disposing of the same to the said Luffⁿ Atterbury only, and in such a manner as he thinks proper - As witness my Hand this 6th Day of July, 1770.
> T. Chatterton.
> Witness: James Allen.[1]

The subsequent history of the manuscript is a rather curious one. In a letter dated 18 June 1802 from John Haslewood to G. Dyer (*L*: C.39.h.20), in answer to Dyer's queries about the authenticity of *The Revenge*, Haslewood notes:

> The MS. Copy of the Revenge was purchased by Mr King of the late Mr. Luffman Atterbury of Abington, Westminster for 5 Guineas. It was afterwards given to the late John Egerton in order to be published and from the information of MʳK I understand the MS. was lost, or supposed to be lost at the Printing House.

A somewhat different account comes from what seems to be a clipping from a Sotheby Sale Catalogue (in *L*: C.39.h.20):

> The Revenge . . . 1795. $4^o$. Chatterton received five guineas for this Burletta from Mr. Luffman Atterbury, one of the proprietors

[1]Meyerstein, p. 402.

> of Marybone Gardens, by whom it was given to Mr. John Egerton, the
> bookseller, who undertook the superintendance of the piece at press.
> The manuscript was supposed to be lost; but Mr. Upcott has it.
> The printed copies, in consequence of the death of the editor, were
> not published.

William Upcott claimed that he had discovered the manuscript in the shop of
a City cheesemonger! The manuscript was purchased by the British Library and
is now Add. MS. 12050.

This, the only separate printing of *The Revenge*, has as its copytext
the British Library manuscript and has no separate authority except for lines
144-96, which are missing from the holograph.

THE | REVENGE, | A BURLETTA; | ACTED AT | MARYBONE GARDENS, | MDCCLXX. |
WITH ADDITIONAL SONGS. | [*double rule*] | *By THOMAS CHATTERTON.* | [*double
rule*] | LONDON: | PRINTED BY C. ROWORTH; | FOR T. KING, KING-STREET,
COVENT-GARDEN; | H. CHAPMAN, WOODSTOCK-STREET; | AND J. EGERTON, WHITE
HALL. | MDCCXCV.

*Collation:* 8° in 4s. [A]$^2$ (A1+X1) B-F$^4$ G$^2$ [$1 (-A1) signed]; 25 leaves, pp.
*1-2* [*2*] *3-4 5-39 40-41 42-48.*

*Contents:* A1$^a$: title (verso blank); X1$^a$: *'Advertisement.* | <u>THIS</u> Burletta,
and the Songs which | follow it, were printed from an original | manu
script in the hand-writing of the | celebrated <u>CHATTERTON</u>, who receiv- |
ed five guineas for the compofition | from the Proprietors of Marybone
Gar- | dens, July 6, 1770. | The manuscript is now in the poffef- | fion
of Mr. <u>LUFFMAN ATTERBURY</u>. | [*double rule*] | SOLD BY | BROWNLOW WAIGHT,
BERNER's STREET, | OXFORD STREET.' (verso blank); A2$^a$: 'CONTENTS.'; A2$^b$:
'DRAMATIS PERSONAE.'; B1$^a$: 'THE | REVENGE.'; F2$^b$ blank; F3$^a$: 'SONGS.';
G2$^b$ blank.

RT] THE REVENGE, | A BURLETTA. B1$^b$
SONGS. F3$^b$

*Typography:* 25 ll. (C4$^a$), 128(143) x 75mm., 80R.; in verse, not divided.
*Notes:* 1. The insert (X1) is printed on different paper and with a different type fount from that used in the rest of the volume.
2. There are small decorative head- and tail-pieces throughout.
*Copies examined:* L (161.h.2; 643.g.7 (6); C.39.f.4; Ashley 2806).

## 16. GARDNER, MISCELLANIES IN PROSE AND VERSE (BRISTOL: BIGGS & COTTLE, 1798)

MISCELLANIES, | IN | PROSE AND VERSE, | BY | *EDWARD GARDNER,* | [*double
rule*] | VOL. I. | [*double rule*] | BRISTOL: | *PRINTED BY BIGGS & COT
TLE,* | And sold by LEE & HURST, Paternoster-Row, LONDON; | BULL, Bath;
COTTLE, and BULGIN & SHEPPARD, Bristol; | HOUGH, and WASHBOURN, Glo
cester; HARWARD, Chelten- | ham; JENNER, Stroud; and BENCE, Wootten-
Underedge. | 1798.

THE

REVENGE,

A BURLETTA;

ACTED AT

MARYBONE GARDENS,

MDCCLXX.

WITH ADDITIONAL SONGS.

By *THOMAS CHATTERTON.*

LONDON:

PRINTED BY C. ROWORTH;

FOR T. KING, KING-STREET, COVENT-GARDEN;
H. CHAPMAN, WOODSTOCK-STREET;
AND J. EGERTON, WHITEHALL.

MDCCXCV.

Fig. VIII. Title page of *The Revenge*, 1795

. 2:   [as in vol. 1, except for volume number; identical type-setting]

*Collation:   v. 1:*  $12^O$ in 6s.  $[\pi]^4$ A-T$^6$ V$^2$, 114 leaves, pp. *i-viii*, 1-232;  *v. 2:*  $[\pi]^3$ A-O$^6$ P$^2$, 89 leaves, pp. *i-vi*, 1-172.

*Selections of Chatterton in v. 2:*   M5$^a$-P1$^b$

*Notes:*    1.  Gardner reprints (2, pp. 159-70) from the *European Magazine* (1791-92) the following Chatterton poems: 'To Miss C---, On Hearing Her Play on the Harpsichord', 'To Mr. Powell', 'Clifton' and 'To Miss Hoyland' ("Sweet are thy charming smiles, my lovely maid,").

*Copies examined:*   L (1208.f.4); B (B.10397).

It was not until thirty years after Chatterton's death that any attempt was made to assemble the poet's entire works to form the basis of a
collected edition.[1]  When Robert Southey and Joseph Cottle decided to under-
take this ambitious endeavour, the former editor advertised the proposed
publication almost immediately:

> The edition will comprize whatever Chatterton left.  Miscellanies,
> the pieces attributed to Rowley, and the letters published by Mr.
> C[roft]; some unpublished poems have been procured, and some mag-
> azine pieces which had escaped the collector of the Miscellanies.
> Dr. Gregory has promised to adapt the life of this extraordinary
> young man to the work; it will make two octavo volumes.  The price
> sixteen shillings, the money to be paid on delivery.  Mr. Kearsly
> receives subscriptions.  The edition will be under my direction,
> and every care shall be taken to render it correct and complete.[2]

The subscription, however, did not progress as well as Southey and
Cottle had hoped and following the publication they were obliged to report
that

> after using every endeavour for two years, it was found that the
> number of Subscribers was not sufficient to defray the expences
> of the proposed edition; . . . Messrs Longman and Rees . . . under-
> took to print it at their own expence, and to allow Mrs. Newton
> 350 copies *gratis*, for her own Subscribers, with a revisionary in-
> terest of 50 copies on the sale of every succeeding edition.[3]

---

[1]A complete edition of Chatterton's works had been desiderated by a
correspondent signing himself 'Juvenis' in *GM*, 57 (Dec. 1787), pp. 1058-59.

[2]*MM*, 8 (Nov. 1799), p. 722.  Southey had previously exposed the treatment of Chatterton's mother and his sister, Mrs. Mary Newton, at the hands of
Sir Herbert Croft in a letter to *MM*, 8 (Nov. 1799) pp. 770-72.  It appears
Croft had published Chatterton's letters without the express permission of the
family.  The letters, which he had borrowed 'for one hour' but did not return
until months later, appeared in his book *Love and Madness* (London 1780).  Southey's estimate of two volumes was to prove inadequate: the edition was eventually
published in three volumes.

[3]*GM*, 74 (1804), p. 722.  Meyerstein, p. 495, notes that the edition
was sold to subscribers at £1 8s and to others at a guinea and a half.

On the whole, the edition has little independent textual authority and is (to use Meyerstein's words) more 'a monument of charity than of intelligent respect'. Affixed to the table of contents of each volume is the following statement: *The Pieces to which Asterisks are prefixed are now first collected or printed.* In the first volume they total thirty-six: twenty-four from manuscripts in Chatterton's handwriting, two from copies in Sir Herbert Croft's hand and three from that author's *Love and Madness*, five from copies in George Catcott's hand, one from the *Town and Country Magazine* and one for which no source is given. There are ten pieces for the first time collected or printed in the second volume: six are printed from manuscripts in the poet's handwriting and four from William Barrett's *History of Bristol*. In the third volume there are sixty-six pieces whose titles are asterisked: thirty-six are taken from Barrett's *History*, twenty-two from manuscripts in Chatterton's hand, five from periodicals, one from Horace Walpole's *Anecdotes of Painting* and two for which no sources are given. Generally, there are notes prefixed to the various pieces in the edition indicating the sources from which they were drawn.

Among the three hundred thirty-five subscribers listed in the first volume are George Catcott, Samuel Taylor Coleridge, the Duchess of Devonshire, the Countess of Granard, Joseph Haslewood, the Countess of Kingston, the Earl and Countess of Moira, La Princesse Joseph de Monaco and the Earl and Countess of Oxford.

*Half-title in each volume:*

   *v. 1:*   The Works | of | Thomas Chatterton. | [*double rule*] | VOL. I. | [*double rule*]

   *v. 2:*   [as in vol. I except for volume number; identical type-setting]

   *v. 3:*   [as in vol. I except for volume number; identical type-setting]

*Volume title in each volume:*

   *v. 1:*   THE | WORKS | OF | THOMAS CHATTERTON. | [*double rule*] | VOL. I. | [*double rule*] | CONTAINING | *HIS LIFE, BY G. GREGORY, D. D.* | AND | *MISCELLANEOUS POEMS.* | [*double rule*] | LONDON: | PRINTED BY BIGGS AND COTTLE, | Crane–Court, Fleet–Street, | FOR T. N. LONGMAN AND O. REES, | PATERNOSTER–ROW. | [*single rule*] | 1803.

   *v. 2:*   [as in vol. I except for volume number and '*THE POEMS ATTRIBUTED TO* | *ROWLEY.*' instead of '*HIS LIFE, BY G. GREGORY, D. D.* | AND | *MIS CELLANEOUS POEMS.*'; identical type-setting]

   *v. 3:*   [as in vol. I except for volume number and '*MISCELLANEOUS PIECES,* | IN | *PROSE.*' instead of '*HIS LIFE, BY G. GREGORY, D. D.* | AND | *MIS CELLANEOUS POEMS.*'; identical type-setting]

*Colophon:*   *v. 1:* $2B2^b$: [*double rule*] | London: Printed by BIGGS & COTTLE, Crane–Court, Fleet–Street.

   *v. 2:* on $2M4^b$: [*double rule*] | Printed by BIGGS & COTTLE, Crane–Court, Fleet–Street.

   *v. 3:* on $2M8^b$: [as in vol. 2]

*Collation:*   $8^o$. *v. 1:* [a]$^2$ b–c$^4$ B–L$^8$ $^2$B–S$^8$ $^2$T$^7$ $^2$U–Z$^8$ 2A$^4$ 2B$^2$, 271 leaves, pp. [20] i–clx, 1-155 *156-58* 159-225 *226-28* 229-362; *v. 2:* [A]$^4$ B–2L$^8$ 2M$^4$, 272 leaves, pp. [8] *1-3* 4-536 [misprinting 224 as 204]; *v. 3:* [A]$^4$ B–2M$^8$, 276 leaves, pp. [8] 1-544 [misprinting 495 as 496 and 496 as 495]

*Contents:*   *v. 1:*   a1$^a$: half-title (verso blank); a2$^a$: volume title (verso blank); b1$^a$: 'PREFACE.'; b2$^b$ blank; b3$^a$: 'CONTENTS.'; b4$^b$ blank; c1$^a$: 'SUBSCRIBERS.'; B1$^a$: 'THE | LIFE | OF | *THOMAS CHATTERTON.*'; $^2$B1$^a$: text; 2B2$^b$: colophon.

   *v. 2:*   A1$^a$: half-title (verso blank); A2$^a$: volume title (verso blank); A3$^a$: 'CONTENTS.'; A4$^b$ blank; B1$^a$: text; 2L4$^b$: 'GLOSSARY.'

   *v. 3:*   A1$^a$: half-title (verso blank); A2$^a$: volume title (verso blank); A3$^a$: 'CONTENTS.'; B1$^a$: text; 2G5$^b$ blank; 2G6$^a$: '*LETTER from Mrs. NEWTON,* | *To the Author of "Love and Madness."*'; 2H1$^b$: '*LETTER from Mr. THISTLETHWAITE,* | *To Dr. Milles, Dean of Exeter.*'; 2I1$^a$: '*LETTER* | *From Mr. T. Cary to Mr.*

G. Catcott.'; 2I2$^a$: 'TESTIMONY | Of Mr. William Smith, concerning Chat
terton.'; 2I3$^b$: 'TESTIMONY | Of Mr. John Rudhall, concerning Chatterton.';
2I8$^a$: 'ANECDOTE | Of CHATTERTON'S FATHER.'; 2I8$^b$: 'A CATCH for Three
Voices.'; 2K1$^a$: 'ACCOUNT of ROWLEY's MSS.'; 2L5$^a$: 'EXTRACT | From Gard
ner's Miscellanies. | Published in 1798.'; 2L5$^b$: 'EXTRACT of a LETTER |
From Mr. Gardner.'; 2L6$^b$: 'LETTER from Mrs. NEWTON.'; 2L7$^b$: 'A COMPLETE
LIST | Of the various Publications incidental to the Works of | CHATTER
TON, and upon the subject of the Poems | attributed to ROWLEY, for and
against their authen- | ticity.'; 2M5$^b$: 'DIRECTIONS for placing the COP
PER-PLATES.'; 2M6$^a$: 'POETICAL WORKS, | Printed for LONGMAN and REES.'

*ypography:* v. 1: 22(24) ll.(F1$^a$), 133(154) x 88mm., 120R.; verse measure,
89mm. (E4$^a$); notes in italics; some black-letter throughout; v. 2: 32
ll. (2K7$^a$), 145(165) x 88mm.; 120R.; verse measure, 83mm. (K7$^a$); notes
in italics; some black-letter throughout; mrg. nn. to 'The Account of
the De Bergham Family'; glossary in double columns; v. 3: 23 ll. (F1$^a$),
139(155) x 89mm., 127R.; notes in italics; some black-letter throughout.

*lates:* v. 1: Facing a2$^a$: 'The Base of the Tower of Redcliff Church, with a
view of the Muniment Room over the North Porch. | Published for Longman
& Rees, Dec.$^n$ 13, 1802.'; lower left corner: 'G. Holmes, del.'; lower
right corner: 'W. Hawkins sc.' (188 x 120mm.).

v. 2: Facing A2$^a$: 'Interior of the Room in Redcliff Church where Rowley's
Manuscripts were said to have been deposited. | Published for Longman &
Rees, Dec.$^n$ 13, 1802.'; lower left corner: 'King del.'; lower right corner: 'Storer sculp.' (186 x 122mm.).
Facing 2G3$^a$: 'THE DE BERGHAM ARMS. | From a Drawing by Chatterton, in
the Possession of M.$^r$ Cottle. | Bye & Smith sc. | Published by T. Longman
& O. Rees, Pater-Noster Row, Nov. 1. 1802.' (154 x 120mm.).
Facing 2K5$^a$: 'CHATTERTON'S ARMS.'; below: 'Smith & Bye sc. | Published
by Longman & Rees, Nov. 1. 1802.' (205 x 120mm.).

v. 3: Facing A2$^a$: 'Fac-simile of Rowley's Hand Writing' and 'Fac-simile of
Chatterton's Hand Writing'; inscribed below: 'Published Jan. 1 1803 by
Longman & Rees Paternoster Row. Neele sculp Strand.' (197 x 118mm.).
Facing G5$^a$: 'SAXON ACHIEVEMENTS.'; below: 'Published Jan. 1 1803 by Long
man & Rees Paternoster Row. Neele sculp Strand.' (202 x 115mm.).
Facing 2K1$^a$: 'Bristol Castle, | 1138.'; lower left corner: 'Rowleie |
delin. 1440. | Published Jan. 1. 1803 by Longman & Rees Paternoster Row.'

(313 x 257mm.; folded).

*Reviewed:*   *ER* (Sir Walter Scott), 4 (Apr. 1804), pp. 214–30; *GM*, 74 (Aug. 1804), p. 722; *GN&Q*, 2 (1884), pp. 599–600; *MMr*, 16 (Oct. 1803), pp. 238–39.

*Copies examined:*   *L* (97.b.22–24; C.39.f.13–15; 12275.aa.27); *O* (8$^O$.E.292–4 BS); *HD* (facsimile reprint by AMS Press, Inc., New York, 1966, of a copy in the Harvard College Library).

# D U B I A

## 18. An Elegy on William Beckford (London: G. Kearsly, 1770)

*Half-title:*   AN | ELEGY, | On the Much Lamented DEATH of | WILLIAM BECKFORD, Efq. | [*single rule*] | [PRICE ONE SHILLING.]

*Title:*   AN | ELEGY | On the Much Lamented DEATH of | WILLIAM BECKFORD, Efq. | Late LORD-MAYOR of, | AND | REPRESENTATIVE in PARLIAMENT | FOR, | THE CITY OF LONDON. | [*single rule*] | *Titles to him no Pleafure could im part,* | *No Bribes his rigid Virtue could controul;* | *The Star could never gain upon his Heart,* | *Nor turn the Tide of Honor in his Soul.* | Vide the Poem. | [*single rule*] | LONDON: | Printed for G. KEARSLY at No. I. in Ludgate-Street. | M.DCC.LXX.

  *Collation:*   4$^O$ in 2s. [A]$^1$ [B]$^2$ C–D$^2$ E$^1$ [\$1 (–A1, B1, E1) signed]; 8 leaves, pp. *1–4* 5–14 *15–16*.

*Contents:*   A1$^a$: half-title (verso blank); B1$^a$: title (verso blank); B2$^a$: text; E1$^a$:'[*single rule*] | *This Day is Publifhed, Price 2s.* | THE AUC TION, A POEM,; a familiar Epiftle to a | Friend, fent with the Head of HARPOCRATES the God of | Silence, in a Ring. | [*single rule*]' (verso blank).

HT]   AN | ELEGY | On the Much Lamented DEATH of | WILLIAM BECKFORD, Efq. B2$^a$
CW]   C1$^a$ Hence [Hence,]   D1$^b$ And [And,]
*Typography:*   15 ll. 178(211) x 131mm. (D2$^a$), 175R.; in verse.

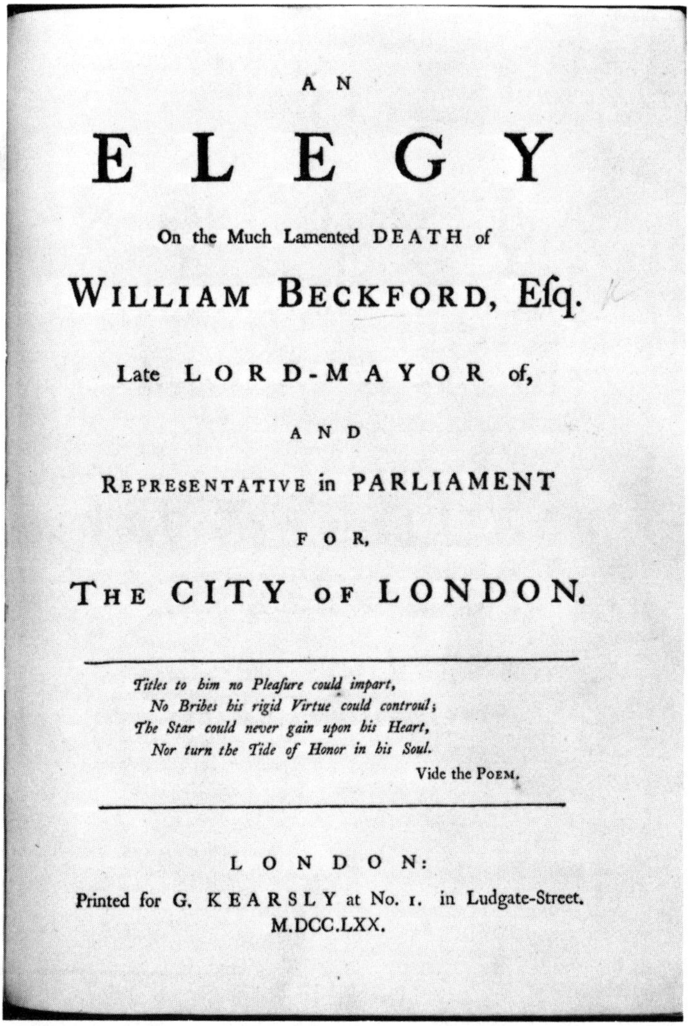

A N

# E L E G Y

On the Much Lamented DEATH of

## WILLIAM BECKFORD, Eſq.

Late L O R D - M A Y O R of,

A N D

REPRESENTATIVE in PARLIAMENT

F O R,

## THE CITY OF LONDON.

---

*Titles to him no Pleaſure could impart,*
*No Bribes his rigid Virtue could controul;*
*The Star could never gain upon his Heart,*
*Nor turn the Tide of Honor in his Soul.*

Vide the POEM.

---

L O N D O N:

Printed for G. K E A R S L Y at No. 1. in Ludgate-Street.
M.DCC.LXX.

Fig. IX.  Title page of *Elegy on William Beckford*, 1770

T H E

A U C T I O N

A

P O E M:

A

FAMILIAR EPISTLE

TO A FRIEND,

With the head of HARPOCRATES, the God of Silence
amongſt the Egyptians, in a Ring.

L O N D O N:

Printed for GEORGE KEARSLY, at N° 1, Ludgate-ſtreet.
MDCCLXX.

Fig. X.  Title page of *The Auction*, 1770

## 9. THE AUCTION (LONDON: G. KEARSLY, 1770)

THE | AUCTION | A | POEM: | A | FAMILIAR EPISTLE | TO A FRIEND, | With
the head of <u>HARPOCRATES</u>, the God of Silence | amongſt the Egyptians, in
a Ring. | [*double rule*] | LONDON: | Printed for <u>GEORGE</u> <u>KEARSLY</u>, at Nᵒ I,
Ludgate-ſtreet. | M DCC LXX.

*Collation:*  4ᵒ.  [A]² B-F⁴ G²  [$2 (-A1, A2, G2) signed]; 24 leaves, pp.
*i-ii* iii-iv, 1-44.

*Contents:*  A1ᵃ: title (verso blank); A2ᵃ: 'ADVERTISEMENT.'; B1ᵃ: text.

T]  A | FAMILIAR EPISTLE | TO A FRIEND, &c.  B1ᵃ

W]  G2ᵃ And  ["And]

*Typography:*  20 ll. 160(178) x 130mm. (G1ᵃ), 160R.; verse measure, 127mm.
(F1ᵃ); in prose and verse, not divided.

*Copies examined:*  L (T.654).

ROWLEY CONTROVERSY

ANON.]   *An Archaeological Epistle to the Reverend and Worshipful Jere-*
*iah Milles, D. D. Dean of Exeter, President of the Society of Antiquar-*
*es, and Editor of a Superb Edition of the Poems of Thomas Rowley, Priest.*
*o which is annexed a Glossary, extracted from that of the Learned Dean.*
*rinted for J. Nichols and others.* London: 1782.

> Preface, dated 15 March 1782, satirizes the orthography of the
> *Rowley Poems*, followed by a parody of Rowley in 21 six-line stan-
> zas entitled, 'Epistelle to Doctoure Mylles'. The 'Epistelle'
> first appeared in the *Public Advertiser* in three parts: Part I:
> 23 March; Part II: 29 March; Part III: 30 March 1782. Its author-
> ship was attributed to William Mason (*GM*, 86 (June 1816), pp. 489-
> 90), but it was more probably written by John Baynes. It was re-
> viewed in: *CR*, 54 (July 1782), pp. 19-22; *GM*, 52 (March 1782), p.
> 129; *MR*, 66 (Apr. 1782), pp. 294-98. A second edition appeared
> in the same year.

ANON.]   *An Examination of the Poems attributed to Thomas Rowley and*
*illiam Canynge. With a Defence of the Opinion of Mr. Warton.* Sher-
orne: R. Goadby & Co., [1782].

> Reviewed in: *CR*, 53 (June 1782), pp. 417-18; *MR*, 67 (Sept. 1782),
> p. 235.

ANON.]   *The Genuine Copy of a Letter Found Nov. 5, 1782, near Straw-*
*erry Hill. Twickenham. Addressed to the Hon. Mr. H----ce W----le.*
ondon: S. Bladon, 1783.

> Satirical review of the Rowley controversy, with reference to the
> various participants. References to Chatterton's acknowledged
> poems as 'the wretched trash of this boy'. Reviewed in: *MR*, 68
> (March 1783), p. 222.

RYANT, JACOB.   *Observations upon the Poems of Thomas Rowley: in which*
*he Authenticity of those Poems is ascertained.* London: T. Payne & Son,
. Cadell, and P. Elmsly, 1781.

> Reviewed in: *CR*, 54 (July-Aug. 1782), pp. 81-98; *EM* (Jan. 1782),
> pp. 34-35; *GM*, 52 (Jan. 1782), pp. 27-28; *MR*, 66-67 (June-July
> 1782), pp. 433-41, 36-46.

COTTLE, JOSEPH. 'On Chatterton and the Rowleian Controversy', in *Malvern Hills, with Minor Poems and Essays*. Fourth Edition. London: T. Cadell, 1829. Two volumes.

> Three essays in vol. 2: 'On Chatterton and the Rowleian Controversy', pp. 382-95; 'On Rowley's Original Manuscripts', pp. 396-409; 'On Chatterton's Armorial Bearings', pp. 410-32. Illustrations at pp. 382, 396, 413, 424. The earlier editions of this work contained no references to Chatterton.

CROFT, SIR HERBERT. *Love and Madness. A Story too True in a Series of Letters Between Parties, whose Names would perhaps be mentioned, were they less known, or lamented*. London: Pt. for G. Kearsly, 1780.

> Letter 49 (pp. 125-244) contains a valuable contribution to the Rowley controversy in favour of Chatterton's authorship.

[DAMPIER, HENRY] *Remarks upon the Eighth Section of the Second Volume of Mr. Warton's History of English Poetry*. London: T. Payne & Son, [1779].

> In support of the authenticity of the Rowley Poems.

GARDNER, EDWARD. 'Original Poems of the late unfortunate Thomas Chatterton, to which is prefixed a short sketch of the controversy concerning the poems attributed to Rowley', in *Miscellanies in Prose and Verse*. Bristol: Biggs & Cottle, 1798. Two volumes.

> Poems and sketch in vol. 2, pp. 141-70.

GREENE, EDWARD BURNABY. *Strictures upon a Pamphlet intitled, Cursory Observations on the Poems attributed to Rowley, A Priest of the Fifteenth Century. With a Postscript on Mr. Thomas Warton's Enquiry into the same subject*. London: J. Stockdale, 1782.

> Dedicatory verses to Dean Percy are signed Edward Burnaby Greene. Reviewed in: *CR*, 54 (July 1782), pp. 25-25; *MR*, 67 (Sept. 1782), p. 235.

GREGORY, GEORGE. *The Life of Thomas Chatterton, with Criticisms on his Genius and Writings, and a Concise View of the Controversy concerning Rowley's Poems.* London: G. Kearsly, 1789.

> Reviewed in: *GM*, 59 (June 1789), pp. 537-38; *MR*, 81 (Oct. 1789), pp. 344-51; *LR* (Nov. 1789), pp. 320-28.

HARDINGE, GEORGE. *Rowley and Chatterton in the Shades: or, Nugae Antiquae et Novae. A new Elysian Interlude, In Prose and Verse.* London: T. Becket, 1782.

> This Interlude, in two acts, features an imaginary meeting between Chatterton and Rowley. Ossian, characters associated with the Rowley Poems, early poets and other dignitaries are introduced as part of a grand illusion. Reviewed in: *CR*, 54 (July 1782), pp. 25-28; *MR*, 67 (Sept. 1782), pp. 235-36.

—————————.' *The Genius of Chatterton, an Irregular Ode Written on the supposition of his being the Author of the Poems attributed to Thomas Rowley in the Fifteenth Century.* London: T. Becket, 1788.

> Reprinted, with a few corrections, from an Interlude at pp. 39-41 of *Rowley and Chatterton in the Shades.*

[HICKFORD, RAYNER] *Observations on the Poems attributed to Rowley, tending to prove that they were really written by Him and other ancient Authors. To which are added Remarks on the Appendix of the Editor of Rowley's Poems by John Fell.* London: Pt. for C. Bathurst, [1782].

> Reviewed in: *CR*, 54 (July 1782), pp. 22-24; *MR*, 67 (Sept. 1782), pp. 234-35.

KNOX, VICESIMUS. 'On the Poems attributed to Rowley', in *Essays Moral and Literary, by Vicesimus Knox, M. A. A New Edition.* London: Pt. for Charles Dilly, 1782. Two volumes.

> Vol. 2, Essay No. 145, pp. 247-51. These Essays went through 17 editions. Also at the same pages, vol. 2, of the 1785 and 1791 editions; at pp. 239-42 of the 1793 edition; and in vol. 3 of the 1787, 1800 and 1808 editions at pp. 205-10, 149-54 and 132-37

respectively. The essay, which did not appear in the first or
the second editions (1778; 1779), pays tribute to Chatterton as
the author of the Rowley Poems and accuses the public of malice
towards him. See *GM*, 59 (July-Aug. 1789), pp. 602-03, 684, 707.


MALONE, EDMOND, *Cursory Observations on the Poems attributed to Thomas
Rowley, A Priest of the Fifteenth Century: with some Remarks on the Com-
mentaries on those Poems, by the Rev. Dr. Jeremiah Milles, Dean of Exeter,
and Jacob Bryant, Esq., and a Salutary Proposal Addressed to the Friends
of those Gentlemen.* Second Edition. Revised and Augmented. London: J.
Nichols, 1782.

> Most of this pamphlet appeared in *GM*, 51 (Dec. 1781), pp. 555-59,
> 609-15. Reviewed in: *CR*, 53 (June 1782), pp. 418-19; *GM*, 52
> (March 1782), p. 128; *MR*, 67 (Sept. 1782), p. 235.


[MANGIN, EDWARD] *A Letter to the "Admirers of Chatterton" by the Author
of "An Essay on Light-Reading".* Bath: Mary Meyler and Son, 1838.

> Dismisses Chatterton as the author of the Rowley Poems.


MATHIAS, THOMAS JAMES, *An Essay on the Evidence, External and Internal,
relating to the Poems attributed to Thomas Rowley. Containing A General
View of the Whole Controversy. By Thomas James Mathias.* London: T.
Becket, 1783.

> Reviewed in: *En R*, 2 (July 1783), pp. 64-65; *MR*, 70 (March 1783),
> pp. 221-22. A second edition appeared in 1784.


MILLES, JEREMIAH, 'A Commentary, in which the Antiquity of them [*i.e.*
Rowley Poems] is considered and defended', in *Poems, supposed to have
been written at Bristol by Thomas Rowley.* London: T. Payne and Son,
1782 [1781]. *Qv.* No. 7.


PERIODICALS:

ANNUAL REGISTER, 'An Account of the Finding or Forging of some very ingenious Poems attributed to Thomas Rowley, a Priest of Bristol, in the

Fifteenth Century, and others of his Fellow-Citizens and Contemporaries; and of the Pieces themselves, as well as the very extraordinary Person who first produced them; being the Preface, Table of Contents, Introductory Account, and Advertisement, prefixed to the Collection [*i.e.*, *Rowley Poems*, 1st edition, 1777] of these pieces, new published', 19 (1776), Antiquities, pp. 155-62.

————————. 'A short Account of William Cannings . . . Wrote by the foregoing Thomas Rowlie', *Ibid.*, pp. 162-65.

————————. 'Further Remarks on the supposed Poems, ascribed to Rowlie', 21 (1781), pp. 153-58.

EUROPEAN MAGAZINE, 'Chatterton Redivivus; or the Authenticity of Rowley's Poems irrefragably vindicated', 1 (Apr. 1782), pp. 262-63.

Contains a summary of the main arguments for and against Chatterton's authorship. Uses proper names in 'The Battle of Hastings' as proof of authenticity, making reference to the inaccessibility of the Domesday Book to Chatterton.

GENTLEMAN'S MAGAZINE, 'On Rowlie's Poems, lately discovered in an old Chest found in a Belfry at Bristol by the Parish-Clerk', 47 (May 1777), pp. 205-08.

Objections to authenticity on the grounds of language and terminology.

————————. [Authenticity of Rowley Poems defended in a review of Tyrwhitt's first edition], 47 (June 1777), pp. 275-79.

The reviewer stresses, 'We can by no means suppose that one so young, so dissipated, so distressed as Chatterton . . . was equal to the composition of such finished pieces'.

————————. [Letter signed 'Crito' in answer to an 'Objector to the Authenticity of Rowley's Poems'], 47 (June 1777), p. 317.

'Crito' protests that arrows shot up into the air, as happens in 'The Battle of Hastings', being 'large and heavy, and acquiring weight by their fall, are formidable weapons, and lighting on the head, seldom fail to do execution'.

GENTLEMAN'S MAGAZINE, [Correspondence concerning the authenticity of
the Rowley Poems], 47 (July-Aug. 1777), pp. 305-07, 361-65.

In the first letter the Poems are dismissed as spurious, though
not lacking in merit and George Catcott's essay (*MR*, May 1777)
is accused of inconsistency.  In the second the Poems are found
to be spurious on literary grounds, but are praised for their
intrinsic merit.

——————————. [Fragment of a sermon presented as further proof of
Rowley's authenticity], 47 (Sept. 1777), pp. 413-14.

'A.B.' writes, 'It may be necessary to inform you, that, when
Chatterton gave this fragment to his friend [George Catcott],
he was utterly (and ever after continued) unacquainted with any
language but his mother-tongue.'

——————————. [Concerning the authenticity of Rowley's Poems], 47
(Oct. 1777), pp. 481-82.

Pronounces Rowley's 'Memoirs of William Canynge' a forgery and
calls upon William Barrett in his researches for the proposed
*History of Bristol* 'to leave no stone unturned till he has drag-
ged the impostor into open day'.

——————————. [Postscript of a letter signed 'H. A. A.' giving evidence that Rowley's Poems are not ancient], 48 (July 1778), p. 314.

Knitted stockings, mentioned in 'Elinoure and Juga', did not appear until the reign of Elizabeth I.

——————————. [Letter from George Catcott in defence of the antiquity of the Rowley Poems, objecting to statements in Warton's *History
of English Poetry*], 48 (Aug. 1778), pp. 347-48.

——————————. 'Rowley unknown to William of Worcester', 50 (Nov.
1780), p. 513.

——————————. [Remarks by 'Misopiclerus' (*i.e.*, Edmond Malone) on two
new publications on Rowley's Poems], 51 (Dec. & Suppl. 1781), pp. 555-
59, 609-15.

The two publications referred to are Milles' edition of the *Rowley
Poems* and Bryant's *Observations upon the Poems of Rowley*.

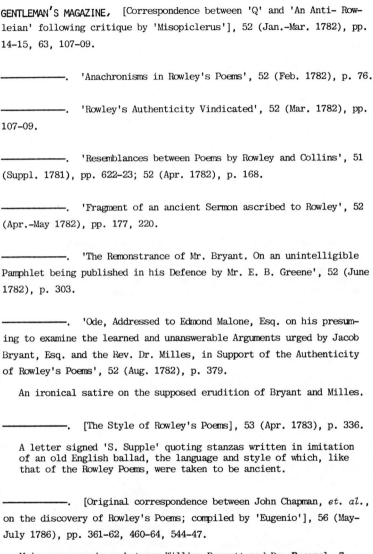

GENTLEMAN'S MAGAZINE, [Correspondence between 'Q' and 'An Anti- Row- leian' following critique by 'Misopiclerus'], 52 (Jan.-Mar. 1782), pp. 14-15, 63, 107-09.

—————. 'Anachronisms in Rowley's Poems', 52 (Feb. 1782), p. 76.

—————. 'Rowley's Authenticity Vindicated', 52 (Mar. 1782), pp. 107-09.

—————. 'Resemblances between Poems by Rowley and Collins', 51 (Suppl. 1781), pp. 622-23; 52 (Apr. 1782), p. 168.

—————. 'Fragment of an ancient Sermon ascribed to Rowley', 52 (Apr.-May 1782), pp. 177, 220.

—————. 'The Remonstrance of Mr. Bryant. On an unintelligible Pamphlet being published in his Defence by Mr. E. B. Greene', 52 (June 1782), p. 303.

—————. 'Ode, Addressed to Edmond Malone, Esq. on his presum- ing to examine the learned and unanswerable Arguments urged by Jacob Bryant, Esq. and the Rev. Dr. Milles, in Support of the Authenticity of Rowley's Poems', 52 (Aug. 1782), p. 379.

An ironical satire on the supposed erudition of Bryant and Milles.

—————. [The Style of Rowley's Poems], 53 (Apr. 1783), p. 336.

A letter signed 'S. Supple' quoting stanzas written in imitation of an old English ballad, the language and style of which, like that of the Rowley Poems, were taken to be ancient.

—————. [Original correspondence between John Chapman, et. al., on the discovery of Rowley's Poems; compiled by 'Eugenio'], 56 (May- July 1786), pp. 361-62, 460-64, 544-47.

Main correspondence between William Barrett and Dr. Ducarel, 7 March - 30 July 1772. Authenticity of Rowley originals is firmly asserted by Barrett in discussion of researches for his proposed *History of Bristol*. Dr. Ducarel stresses the need for early pub- lication of Rowley's works. Chapman hopes for a collected edition and deplores the division of pieces between Barrett and Catcott.

GENTLEMAN'S MAGAZINE, 'Rowley's Drawings Spurious', 56 (July 1786), p. 580.

In this extract from a letter to Dr. Ducarel, the anonymous antiquary relates how, on the basis of erroneous inscriptions, he detected that drawings of Roman altars shown him by William Barrett were forgeries.

—————. ['Veritas' defends Catcott and Barrett against derogatory remarks by John Chapman], 56 (Oct. 1786), pp. 859-60.

—————. 'The Rowley Controversy: the Role of Steevens and Tyrwhitt', 58 (Mar. 1788), pp. 187-88.

Steevens and Tyrwhitt vindicated in the face of derogatory remarks by Dr. Johnson.

—————. 'The Rowley Controversy' *in* 'Anecdotes of Mr. Badcock; extracted from his letters', 58 (Sept. 1788), p. 781.

Speaks of preparatory work for a review of Milles' edition given in *MR* for March, 1782. Verdict on the Poems: 'My sentiments are fixed. The poems are modern'.

—————. 'The Rowley Controversy' *in* 'Original Anecdotes of Mr. Badcock from his own Letters', 59 (Oct. 1789), pp. 877-78.

Refers to the second part of his review of Milles' edition (*MR*, May 1782). He insists upon his freedom to disagree with his predecessor, Dr. Langhorne, as Editor of *MR*.

—————. [John Sherwen on the Rowley Controversy], 80 (Jan. 1810), pp. 9-11; (May 1810), pp. 411-15.

Sherwen dismisses the anti-Rowleians and announces his intention to publish further on the subject.

—————. [The authenticity of the Rowley Poems defended by John Sherwen], 80 (Sept. 1810), pp. 209-14; 81 (May 1811), pp. 426-28; (June 1811), pp. 513-16; (Aug. 1811), pp. 119-21; (Nov. 1811), pp. 429-32; (Dec. 1811), pp. 523-25.

GENTLEMAN'S MAGAZINE, 'The Antiquity of Rowley's Poems', 80, pt. 1 (Suppl. 1810), pp. 618-19; 81 (Aug. 1811), pp. 121-24.

Comments on Chatterton's fabrication of old English, with reference to a passage from 'The Tournament'.

——————. [Remarks on Rowley's Poems and on Chatterton], 92 (Jan. 1822), pp. 36-39.

Letter signed 'J. S.', [John Sherwen?] in defence of the poems' authenticity, with more references to Chaucer and other early writers.

NEW REVIEW, 'Short Sketch of the Chattertonian Controversy from the Works of Mr. Tyrwhitt, Milles, Bryant, &c.', 1 (Apr. 1782), pp. 218-29.

SCOTS MAGAZINE, 'Remarks on the Controversy respecting the Poems of Rowley', 64 (May 1802), pp. 405-07.

TINSLEY'S MAGAZINE, 'A Difficult Brief: *in re* Chatterton', 30 (May 1882), pp. 441-45.

Critical examination of Jacob Bryant's argument.

——————. 'Chatterton; or the Rowley Romancer', 14 (Apr. 1874), pp. 382-97.

Impartial survey at a safe distance from the controversy.

[RITSON, JOSEPH] *Observations on the first three Volumes of the 'History of English Poetry'. In a familiar Letter to the Author.* London: J. Stockdale & R. Faulder, 1782.

Accuses Warton of ignorance of the subject, and dismisses the work as useless.

SHERWEN, JOHN, *Introduction to an Examination of some part of the internal Evidence, respecting the Antiquity and Authenticity of Certain Publications, said to have been found in Manuscripts, at Bristol, written by a Learned Priest and Others, in the Fifteenth Century; but generally consided (sic.) as the Suppositious Productions of an In-*

*genious Youth of the Present Age.* By John Sherwen, M. D. Bath: Meyler and Son, 1809.

> Belated expression of Rowleian sentiments. Reviewed in: *GM*, 80 (Sept. 1810), pp. 245-48; 81 (Aug. 1811), pp. 121-24; *MR*, 61 (Jan. 1810), pp. 35-43.

TURGOTUS, JOHANNES. *The Prophecy of Queen Emma; An Ancient Ballad lately discovered, written by Johannes Turgotus, Prior of Durham, in the Reign of William Rufus. To which is added, by the Editor, An Account of the Discovery, and Hints towards a Vindication of the Authenticity of the Poems of Ossian and Rowley.* London: Pt. for J. Bew, 1782.

> The editor was Willaim Mickle. Reviewed in: *CR*, 53 (June 1782), pp. 419-21; *MR*, 67 (Sept. 1782), p. 237.

TYRWHITT, THOMAS. 'An Appendix, containing some Observations upon the language of these Poems; tending to prove that they were written, not by any Ancient Author, but entirely by Thomas Chatterton', in *Poems, Supposed to have been written at Bristol, by Thomas Rowley.* London: T. Payne & Son, 1778.

> The Appendix to this, the third edition, is at pp. 309-33.

—————————. *A Vindication of the Appendix to the Poems, called Rowley's, in Reply to the Answers of the Dean of Exeter, Jacob Bryant, Esquire, and a Third Anonymous Writer; with some further Observations upon these Poems, and an Examination of the Evidence which has been produced in support of their Authenticity; by Thomas Tyrwhitt.* London: T. Payne & Son, 1782.

> Detailed examination, in four parts, of the facts and arguments regarding the authorship of the Poems. Reviewed in: *CR*, 54 (Sept. 1782), pp. 186-205; *GM*, 58 (Mar. 1788), pp. 187-88; *MR*, 67 (Oct. 1782), pp. 266-70; *NR*, 2 (Sept. 1782), pp. 229-33.

WARTON, THOMAS. *An Enquiry into the Authenticity of the Poems attributed to Thomas Rowley. In which the Arguments of the Dean of Exeter, and Mr. Bryant are examined. By Thomas Warton.* London: J. Dodsley, 1782.

Anti-Rowleian viewpoint. Reviewed in: *BMR*, (Oct. 1782), pp. 282–91; *CR*, 54 (Aug. 1782), pp. 98–109; *GM*, 52 (Mar.-Apr. 1782), pp. 129–30, 195–97; *MR*, 67 (Sept. 1782), pp. 161–70; *RGL*, (Oct. 1782), pp. 282–91. Another edition appeared in the same year.

WARTON, THOMAS, 'Poems under the name of Thomas Rowlie. Supposed to be Spurious', in *The History of English Poetry*, vol. 2, section 8, pp. 139–64. London: J. Dodsley, 1778. Three volumes.

Anti-Rowleian point of view, with a detailed discussion of the poems. Another edition, published by Thomas Tegg, 1824, is a reprint of the above, with additional new proofs of forgery, but the section relating to the Rowley Poems was omitted from the 1871 edition. Reviewed in: *GM*, 48 (May 1778), pp. 201–02, 226–29, 347–48; 53 (Apr. 1783), p. 281.

CHATTERTON  BIOGRAPHY

# I. BOOKS AND PAMPHLETS

BAYLIS, F. G. *Footprints of Genius: A Biography of Thomas Chatterton, of Bristol.* (Gloucester: Davies and Son, and T. C. Goulding, [1859]).

BENNETT, JAMES R. *The Life of Thomas Chatterton, the Poet.* (Birmingham: J. Dowler, 1860).

> Some verses, said to have been found on the table in Chatterton's room after his death, are printed on the cover.

DAVIS, JOHN. *The Life of Thomas Chatterton.* (London: Thomas Tegg, 1806).

> Reviewed in: *London Review*, 1 (May 1809), pp. 223-54.

DIX, JOHN. *The Life of Thomas Chatterton.* (London: Hamilton, Adams and Co., 1837).

> Contains the first complete printed version of 'Kew Gardens' at pp. 154-94.

ELLINGER, ESTHER P. *Thomas Chatterton, the Marvellous Boy; To which is added 'The Exhibition': A Personal Satire.* (Philadelphia: University of Pennsylvania Press, 1930).

> Most early biographers ascribed Chatterton's urge to forge poetry to genius, the devil or insanity, but Miss Ellinger sees the poet's compulsion as the manifestation of neurotic impulses. From Adler's *The Neurotic Constitution* she extracts the principles of neurosis and they seem to tally to a high degree with the traits attributed to Chatterton's character. The virulent satire, 'The Exhibition', hitherto considered unfit for publication on moral grounds, is here printed as valuable evidence of neurosis.
> Reviewed in: *American Bookman*, 71 (Dec. 1930), pp. 453-54; *MLN*, 46 (June 1931), pp. 417-18; *MLR*, 26 (Oct. 1931), pp. 474-76; *RES*, 8 (Oct. 1932), pp. 496-97; *TLS*, 31 July 1930, p. 625; *YWES*, 11 (1930), pp. 289-90.

ELRINGTON, STEPHEN N. *The Life and Character of Thomas Chatterton: A Lecture.* (Dublin: Alexander Thom, 1864).

ELRINGTON, STEPHEN N.  *The Martyrdom of Misdirected Genius. The Life and Character of Chatterton: A Lecture, delivered before the Dublin Young Men's Christian Association, June, 1864.*  (Dublin: 1864, *pamphlet*).

GEORGE, WILLIAM.  *New Facts Relating to the Chatterton Family; Gathered from Manuscript Entries in a 'History of the Bible' which once belonged to the Parents of Thomas Chatterton, and from Parish Registers.*  (Bristol: W. George and Son, 1883, *pamphlet*).

> Records discovered by John Taylor, Librarian of Bristol Museum and Library.  A reprint of some letters to the *A* (Dec. 1881), pp. 780, 813, 901; (Jan. 1882), pp. 17, 57-58, 94, 125-26; (Feb. 1882), pp. 156-57, 220, 252; and of one to *BT&M*, 20 Feb. 1862.

——————, *Thomas Chatterton and the Vicar of Temple Church, Bristol, A. D. 1768-1770; including the Poet's Account of the 'Knightes Templaries Chyrche'.* (Bristol: William George's Sons, 1888, *pamphlet*).

> Fifty 1p. copies (Demy $4^{O}$) were printed on Whatman paper.  The Vicar was the Reverend Alexander Catcott.

GREGORY, GEORGE.  *The Life of Thomas Chatterton, with Criticisms on his Genius and Writings, and a Concise View of the Controversy Concerning Rowley's Poems.*  (London: G. Kearsley, 1789).

> Reviewed in: *GM*, 59 (June 1789), pp. 537-38; *London Review*, Nov. 1789, pp. 320-28; *MR*, 81 (Oct. 1789), pp. 344-51.  Reprinted in Kippis' *Biographia Britannica*, 3, pp. 573-619 and in the 1803 edition of Chatterton's *Works*.

INGRAM, JOHN HENRY.  *Chatterton and His Poetry.*  (London: George G. Harrap and Co. (Poetry and Life Series, No. 28), 1916).

> Biographical study as the setting for a selection of representative poems.

——————, *The True Chatterton: A New Study from Original Documents.* (London: T. Fisher Unwin, 1910).

A three hundred fifty page biography of which very little was not already recorded in earlier accounts of the poet's life. Much is made of the indiscriminate quotations from well-known poems with Ingram's accompanying comments on them.
Reviewed in: *A*, 27 Aug. 1910, p. 234; *BT&M*, 1 Aug. 1910; *Current Literature*, 49 (Oct. 1910), pp. 448–49; *Nt*, Aug. 1910, pp. 674–75, 707, 740; *SR*, 110 (13 Aug. 1910), pp. 205–06; *WDP*, 20 Aug. 1910.

JENNINGS, HENRY J. *Thomas Chatterton, the Boy Poet of Bristol: a Biographical Sketch.* (Bristol: St. Augustine's Press; London: T. Bosworth, 1868, pamphlet).

KELLY, LINDA. *The Marvellous Boy. The Life and Myth of Thomas Chatterton.* (London: Weidenfeld and Nicolson, 1971).

'Chatterton, starving in his garret, is the precursor of the cult figures of our time - actors, musicians, revolutionaries, whose early death has made them symbols. Youth and death are a powerful combination. In Chatterton's case they were linked to poetic genius. The poetry remains, more lasting than the legend.' Many inaccuracies, particularly in biographical details.
Reviewed in: *TLS*, 25 Aug. 1972, p. 988.

MAITLAND, SAMUEL R. *Chatterton: An Essay.* (London: Rivington, 1857).

The object of the Essay is to correct society's mistake of fancying that Chatterton was anything else but a rather clever but still very ignorant and illiterate rogue. Anything more than that - all talk of his being an unfortunate youth of genius - seems to Maitland to be erroneous.
Reviewed in: *A*, 17 Jan. 1857, pp. 73-76; *SR*, 3 (7 Feb. 1857), pp. 133-35.

MEYERSTEIN, E. H. W. *A Bristol Friendship: Thomas Chatterton and John Baker.* (Royal Society of Literature, Essays by Divers Hands, v. 25, 1950).

The Wedmore Memorial Lecture delivered before the Royal Society of Literature on 30 April 1947. Illustrated by previously unpublished correspondence discovered by Meyerstein.

—————, *A Life of Thomas Chatterton.* (London: Ingpen and Grant, 1930).

Meyerstein, *the* authority on Chatterton's life, gives a very thorough examination and revaluation of the poet and his work. He stresses in particular the importance of the boy's Bristol environment on his development and presents his own view of Chatterton's rejection by Walpole. Many letters are here printed for the first time and throw light on the circumstances of the poet's life and death. In addition the author gives an erudite and concise literary appreciation of the poetry. An indispensable guide to any study of Chatterton.

Reviewed in: *Bk*, 79 (Dec. 1930), p. 197; *BT&M*, 4 Nov. 1930; *Englischen Studien*, 66 (1931-32), pp. 286-87; *MLN*, 47 (Feb. 1932), pp. 122-25; *MLR*, 26 (Oct. 1931), pp. 474-47; *Nt*, 133 (22 July 1931), pp. 93-94; *New Statesman*, 36 (20 Dec. 1930), p. 337; *Quarterly Review*, 256 (Jan. 1931), pp. 198-99; *SR*, 150 (Nov. 1930), pp. 604-16; *Saturday Review of Literature*, 7 (13 June 1931), p. 895; *Spectator*, 15 Nov. 1930, pp. 733-34; *TLS*, 27 Nov. 1930), p. 1009; *Weekend Review*, 2 (11 Dec. 1930), pp. 958-59; *Yale Review*, 21 (Autumn 1931), pp. 207-08; *YWES*, 11 (1930), pp. 288-89.


**NEVIL, JOHN CRANSTOUN,** *Thomas Chatterton*. (London: Frederick Muller, Ltd., 1948).

Reviewed in: *TLS*, 23 Oct. 1948, p. 598; 13 Nov. 1948, p. 639.


**RICHTER, HELENE,** *Thomas Chatterton*. (Vienna: Wiener Beitrage zur englischen Philologie, 1900).


**RUSSELL, CHARLES E,** *Thomas Chatterton, the Marvellous Boy: The Story of a Strange Life, 1752-1770*. (New York: Moffat, Yard and Co., 1908).


**SHEPPERLEY, WILLIAM,** *Chatterton*. (London: Bowyer Press, 1914, *pamphlet*).


**WALPOLE, HORACE,** *A Letter to the Editor of the Miscellanies of Thomas Chatterton*. Strawberry Hill: T. Kirgate, 1779).

A vindication of Walpole's conduct towards Chatterton in the face of public condemnation. Reprinted as 'Walpole's Account of Chatterton', *GM*, 52 (Apr.–July 1782), pp. 189-95, 247-50, 300, 347-48.


**WILSON, DANIEL,** *Chatterton: A Biographical Study*. (London: Macmillan and o., 1869).

Aims to give a more complete and balanced picture than the earlier biographers.
Reviewed in: *A*, 21 May 1881, p. 688; *N&Q*, 4th ser., 5 (7 May 1870), p. 455.

# I. PERIODICALS

ANON.] 'An Interesting Anniversary', *BT&M*, 22 Dec. 1906.

Recalls Chatterton's letter to publisher James Dodsley and the poet's subsequent career in London.

ARNES, WILFRED. 'Chatterton Controversy: Was the boy poet secretly buried t Redcliff?', *Bristol Evening World*, 18 Dec. 1941.

ROWN, T. J. 'Thomas Chatterton, 1752-1770', *Book Collector*, 3 (1954), p. 37.

An examination of Chatterton's handwriting reveals that in his 'antique writing' his letter-forms show that he was consciously trying to imitate a mediaeval hand, 'but the squalid arrangement and near illegibility of his 'original' are never found in any mediaeval document, however private and informal.'

CLARK, F. E. 'Chatterton Sketch', *North American*, 182 (Feb. 1906), pp. 256-58.


DAVIS, BERTRAM R. 'Thomas Chatterton, 1752-1770', *Illustrated Bristol News*, 5 (Sept. 1962), pp. 50-51.

Brief sketch of Chatterton's life.


DEAN, F. R. 'Thomas Chatterton. A Literary Masquerader', *Papers of the Manchester Literary Club*, 63 (1937), pp. 116-28.

General survey of the poet's life that adds nothing new to our knowledge or understanding of Chatterton.


J. W. T. L. 'Thomas Chatterton', *Bristol Daily Mercury*, 28 July 1903.

Covers the period to Chatterton's departure for London.


JAMES, PAULINE K. 'Chatterton's Best Friend: Some Details of William Barrett's Library', *BT&M*, 30 Jan. 1924.

An account of Chatterton's early life and introduction to Barrett.


MABBOTT, T. O. 'Notes on Chatterton: A Letter from Isaac Fell', *N&Q*, 178 (6 Jan. 1940), p. 3

A letter from Isaac Fell requesting that Chatterton forward 'The Resignation' so that Fell might publish it in the *Freeholder's Magazine*, of which he was the editor.


——————, 'Notes on Chatterton: A Letter to William Smith', *N&Q*, 162 (2 Apr. 1932), pp. 242-43.

An examination of the underlying meaning of the letter, the full text of which appears in Meyerstein's *Life* and the light which it sheds on the poet's character.


MEYERSTEIN, E. H. W. 'Chatterton and the Angel', *TLS*, 21 Jan. 1939, p. 42.

The 'Angel', which was engraved on a cup presented to Chatterton when a child, might have had its origin in an engraving of the south prospect of St. Mary Redcliff Church, by James Stewart, 1745. Meyerstein asks, 'Can it be that here we have an earlier date for the genesis of the Rowley myth in the child's mind than the sight of the coffers and their parchments in the muniment room over the north porch?'

EYERSTEIN, E. H. W. 'Chattertoniana', *TLS*, 6 Jan. 1950, p. 9.

Gives the 'true text' of a fragment in Chatterton's autograph of 'The Merrie Tricks of Lamyngetown' acquired by the Bristol Library.

————, 'Chatterton's Infidelity', *TLS*, 2 Apr. 1922, p. 140.

Gives the text of lines by Chatterton, never before printed, found in his autograph on the fly-leaf of a copy of his friend the Rev. Alexander Catcott's *Treatise on the Deluge*. The fragment explains 'the aversion the young poet inspired in his contemporaries, and which, in part, may have led the vicar of Temple Church, Bristol, to break with him'.

————, 'Chatterton's Last Days', *TLS*, 28 June 1941, p. 316.

An investigation of the term 'composing smegma', used by Chatterton in a letter to his friend William Smith about a fortnight before he died. Meyerstein suggests that 'composing' here means 'allaying, alleviating' and recalls Skelton's 'Why come ye not to Court' in which smegma is connected with venereal disease. Meyerstein asks, 'Can it be that this passage was running in Chatterton's mind when he wrote to Smith?'

————, 'Chatterton's Letter from Isaac Fell', *N&Q*, 178 (20 Apr. 1940), 280.

Notes on the 'Ode to Duke Harry' and the reason for its non-publication in the *Freeholder's Magazine*.

————, 'John Baker's Letters to Chatterton', *TLS*, 26 Apr. 1947, p. 04.

Meyerstein records how Baker, a friend of Chatterton who went to South Carolina and subsequently died there, gave his papers, including Chatterton's poems (with an acrostic and an ode) on

Eleanor Hoyland, two on Sally Clark, and 'The Tournament' to
Abraham Lloyd. The editors of Chatterton have been incorrect
in dating the Chatterton letters to Baker covering the above
poems as 'March 6, 1768'. The recovery of the first of two
letters from Baker to Chatterton shows that the year should be
1769.

MEYERSTEIN, E. H. W.    'Thomas Chatterton', *TLS*, 25 June 1931, p. 504.

> Points revealed since the publication of the *Life*, including
> notes on Chatterton's parents, the nature of his death and
> evidence of the suspicion with which Percy regarded the Rowley
> Poems.

MOFFATT, WILLIAM D.    'The World's Most Unfortunate Poet', *The Mentor*, 9
Sept. 1921.

PRICE, J. B.    'Thomas Chatterton, the Hoaxer', *Contemporary Review*, 185
(1954), pp. 95-99.

> General and brief survey of Chatterton's life and works. Adds
> nothing new to the field of Chatterton biography or criticism.

RUSSELL, A. H.    'Chatterton's Birthplace', *BT&M*, 24 and 29 July 1929.

TAYLOR, DONALD S.    'Chatterton's Suicide', *PQ*, 31 (Jan. 1952), pp. 63-69.

> Taylor argues, from the evidence in Chatterton's Memorandum Book,
> that poverty was not the motive for the poet's suicide.

W. B. H.    'Chatterton's Apprenticeship to Lambert', *N&Q*, 12th ser., 8 (5
Feb. 1921), p. 114.

> Quotes from Howitt's *Homes and Haunts of the British Poets* that
> Chatterton's life as an apprentice to Lambert, a lawyer in whose
> employ the boy poet remained until March, 1770, was a 'life of
> insult and degradation'.

WALDHORN, A. 'Thomas Chatterton, de Burgham, and John Dix', *N&Q*, 196 (17 Mar. 1951), pp. 120-21.

> John Dix, a biographer of Chatterton, is suspected of forgery for having included in his book unauthenticated items not written by the same hand that wrote the Rowley Poems.

WALTERS, JOHN. 'Thomas Chatterton, Teenage Amorist', *WDP*, 25-29 Oct. 1965.

WASSERMAN, EARL R. 'The Walpole-Chatterton Controversy', *MLN*, 54 (June 1939), pp. 460-62.

> Wasserman reveals that Isaac Reed, in one of his MS notebooks (Folger MS 632), preserved an account of the Chatterton-Walpole controversy which substantiates Walpole's account of his treatment of the boy as told in his *Letter to the Editor of the Miscellanies of Thomas Chatterton* (1179).

WRIGHT, G. W. 'On Chatterton's Apprenticeship', *N&Q*, 8 (8 Jan. 1921), p. 31.

> Disagrees with Sir Sidney Lee's assertion (*Dictionary of National Biography*) that Chatterton's life as an apprentice to Lambert was harsh and that he was overworked.

——————, 'Thomas Chatterton', *N&Q*, 12th ser, 8 (5 Feb. 1921), p. 108.

> Chatterton's death and burial: special reference to possible interment at Bristol.

——————, 'Thomas Chatterton', *N&Q*, 12th ser, 9 (20 Aug. 1921), pp. 148-49.

> Further discussion of Chatterton's apprenticeship to Lambert, proving from the testimony of Chatterton's family that the boy was not overworked.

LITERARY CRITICISM

[ANON.]    'The Attorney's Clerk in the Monk's Hood', *Blackwood's Magazine*, 53 1843), pp. 780-90.

> General consideration of Chatterton's works with a scathing attack on Walpole for his unkind treatment of the boy. 'It is no unreasonable charity to believe, that what was unworthy and unsound in his character . . . might, under more auspicious circumstances of condition and training, have been kept in check till utterly expelled by the force of his own maturer mind.'

[ANON.]    'Rowley Superior to Homer, Virgil, Spenser and Shakespeare!', *GM*, 52 (Feb. 1782), pp. 62-63.

> Illustrated from passages in Dean Milles' Commentary.

BRONSON, BERTRAND H.    'Chattertoniana', *MLQ*, 11 (Dec. 1950), pp. 417-24.

> Bronson disagrees with Meyerstein's view that Percy's *Reliques* was 'almost the efficient poetical cause of Rowley'. He maintains that the honour more properly belongs to Elizabeth Cooper's *The Muses' Library*, 1737. Although Chatterton did not boldly copy lines or passages from Cooper, Bronson finds many striking similarities 'in tone and temper, in metrics and subjects'. Appended to Bronson's consideration of the problem of Chatterton's sources are further considerations of spellings, word meanings and pronunciations in Chatterton.

——————, 'Thomas Chatterton' in *The Age of Johnson* (New Haven: Yale University Press, [1949]).

> Rowley is seen as a 'father figure' in Chatterton's development as a writer. The depth of experience in the Rowley Poems is contrasted with the immature shallowness in the other works.

BROWNING, ROBERT.    *Essay on Chatterton; Edited with Introductory Chapters and Notes by Donald Smalley.* (Cambridge, Mass.: Harvard University Press, 1948).

> The Essay was first published anonymously in the *Foreign Quarterly Review* for 1842 as a review of R. H. Wilde's *Conjectures and Researches Concerning the Love, Madness, and Imprisonment of Torquato Tasso.* An account of the discovery of the Essay and its authorship may be found in R. D. Altick's *The Scholar Adventurers* (New York:

Macmillan, 1950). Smalley sees the Essay as 'an experiment in the art of special-pleading'.
Reviewed in: *Journal of English and Germanic Philology*, 48 (1949), pp. 299-300; *N&Q*, 194 (1 Oct. 1949), p. 440; *TLS*, 16 Sept. 1949, p. 602; *Victorian Newsletter*, No. 19 (1961), pp. 17-18.

CHAPMAN, R. W. 'Chatterton's *Execution of Sir Charles Bawdin*', *BN&Q*, 1, No. 2 (1935), p. 8.

> Chapman's reply to T. O. Mabbott that it appears one of the title-pages (Goldsmith's) of *The Execution* is an insert.

CLARKE, ERNEST. *New Lights on Chatterton*. (Transactions of the Bibliographical Society, 1916, *pamphlet*).

> Clarke exhibits for the first time a notebook of Dr. Fry, President of St. John's College, Oxford, containing transcripts of some of the Rowley Poems and an uncompleted glossary, the original parchments of 'Aella' and 'The Yellow Roll', documents from the Percy collection, Catcott's notebook of articles written in connection with the Rowley controversy (including the description of Rowley by his master, William Canynge, not found elsewhere) and the original MS. of Horace Walpole's vindication of his conduct towards the poet.
> Reviewed in: *BT&M*, 12 Aug. 1916.

COTTLE, BASIL. *Thomas Chatterton*. (Bristol Branch of the Historical Association: Local History Pamphlets (No. 6), 1963).

> A pointed and penetrating survey in fifteen pages of Chatterton's literary development and the sources from which he drew his inspiration. Cottle claims, '. . . a disservice has been done to the memory of Thomas Chatterton [by] pity and sensationalism; he has been summed up merely as 'the marvellous Boy', his faked mediaeval poems have been examined as a piece of linguistics and not as literature, and Wallis's painting has immortalised the pathos of the juvenile suicide in purple and puce.'

DENNIS, LEAH. 'Chatterton's Rowley Rhymed with 'slowly' in 1778', *Words*, 3 (1937), p. 106.

DIXON, W. MACNEILE. *Chatterton*. (Warton Lecture on English Poetry at the British Academy, 1930, *pamphlet*).

An appreciation of Chatterton's significance as a poet of the imagination in the age of reason. Chatterton's work is viewed against the background of the mediaeval revival.
Reviewed in: *BT&M*, 17 Jan. 1931; *MLN*, 47 (Feb. 1932), pp. 122–25; *MLR*, 26 (Oct. 1931), pp. 474–76; *YWES*, 11 (1930), p. 290.

DGCUMBE, RICHARD, 'Thomas Chatterton', *GM*, 245 (Nov. 1878), pp. 564–79.

An examination of Chatterton's acknowledged productions 'as nearly as possible in the order in which they were written.'

ARRER, JAMES ANSON, 'The Tragedy of Chatterton' in *Literary Forgeries* (London: Longmans, Green and Co., 1907, pp. 145–60.

'When stripped of their garb of pseudo-antiquity and transposed into modern and legible English . . . the Rowley poems are remarkable works, whose production should have entitled Chatterton's memory to more lenient treatment than it ever received.'

ORMAN, H, B, *Thomas Chatterton and His Latest Editor.* (London: Beveridge nd Co., 1874).

Forman praises W. W. Skeat for his handling of the 1871 edition of Chatterton's poetry but takes him to task for not always recording editorial emendations. Forman thinks very highly of the Rowley Poems and predicts that the reading public's final verdict will be that, 'in a large proportion of the Rowley Poems, there is a closer and more genuine love of and adherence to nature than is to be found in the works of the greatest poet [Pope] among those who served Chatterton as models in his eighteenth century work.'

ITTINGS, ROBERT, 'Keats on Chatterton', *K-SJ*, 4 (1955), pp. 47–54.

Gittings traces the chronological development of the influence of Chatterton on Keats' poetry which began in the spring of 1818 and continued until September, 1819.

ORDON, I, A, 'An Unrecorded Copy of Chatterton', *Turnbull Library Record,* lo. 4 (July–Dec. 1941), pp. 6–9.

Gordon records the existence in the Turnbull Library of George

Catcott's copy of Tyrwhitt's third edition of the *Rowley Poems* (1778) in which Catcott's manuscript annotations, augmented by contemporary reviews and articles, show that he was firmly convinced of the authenticity of the poems.

GUTHKE, K. S. 'The Rowley Myth in Eighteenth Century Germany', *PBSA*, 51 (1957), pp. 238–41.

> The development of the Rowley myth in Germany is traced and Guthke reveals how 'the weighty verdict' of J. J. Eschenburg, that the poems were forgeries, silenced all further discussion in that country of the hoax.

HALL, WILLIAM C. 'The Metrical Imitations of Chatterton', *Manchester Quarterly*, No. 83 (July 1902), pp. 267–76.

> Despite the absence of extant poems by Thomas Phillips, Chatterton's teacher, Hall believes that Chatterton probably learned the art of writing poetry from him and may have imitated his pedagogue's style. He notes the resemblance that the 'Songe' in 'The Tragedy of Aella' bears to the mad song of Ophelia, 'Elinoure and Juga' echoes Gray's 'Elegy' and the debt of the Rowley Poems, as regards metrical imitation, to the works of Chaucer and Spenser.

—————, 'The Poetry of Thomas Chatterton', *Manchester Quarterly*, No. 171 (July–Oct. 1924), pp. 187–208.

> An enlightened survey of Chatterton's work, with great praise for his poetic genius. Hall advocates reading the Rowley Poems in their original pseudo– Middle English.

HERMANN, H. 'Dichter oder Fälscher? Thomas Chatterton und die Kraft geschichtlicher Rückerrinnerung in England', *Germania*, No. 308 (1937).

HAZLITT, WILLIAM. 'On Chatterton' in *Lectures on the English Poets* (London: Taylor and Hessey, 1818, pp. 242–44).

> Notes exaggerated praise of Chatterton's work by contemporary writers: 'It is his name, his youth, and what he might have lived to have done, that excite our wonder and imagination.'

LAMOINE, GEORGES, 'La Pensée Religieuse et le Suicide de Thomas Chatterton', *Études Anglais*, 23 (1970), pp. 369-79.

> 'Il ne faut pour autant en déduire que le suicide de Chatterton est la négation de sa croyance; nous inclinons plutôt à penser que ce jeune homme au destin tragique se crut audessus des lois ordinaires humaines et divines, et qu'il concilia l'adhésion à sa religion et sa conception de la liberté.'

LE GRICE, C. V, 'Chatterton and Bailey's Dictionary', *GM*, n.s., 10 (Aug. 1838), pp. 128-33.

> A discussion of Chatterton's probable use of the above in imitating the language of mediaeval poets.

LUND, M. G, 'An Angry Young Man in London: Thomas Chatterton as Satirist', *Forum*, 4 (1922).

——————, 'The Sources of Chatterton's Genius', *University of Kansas City Review*, 25 (1959), pp. 209-17.

> The sources of Chatterton's poetic genius are to be found in his early childhood when he had considered inanimate objects as living beings, in his two years spent in constant reading and wandering about Bristol, in the seven years at Colston's School where he learned to live at will in two worlds and in the three years when 'his soul was tossed between these worlds'.

MABBOTT, T. O, 'Byron and Chatterton: a Parallel', *N&Q*, 162 (19 Mar. 1932), p. 207.

> Byron's opening lines of the 'Monody on Sheridan' ('When the last sunshine of expiring day / On summer's twilight weeps itself away') seems to echo Chatterton's 'Narva and Mored' ('So, when the splendour of the dying day / Darts the mad lustre of the wat'ry way').

——————, 'Chatterton and Byron, a Reminiscence?', *N&Q*, 191 (28 Dec. 1946), p. 281.

> Further consideration of lines from Byron's 'Monody on Sheridan' and Chatterton's 'Narva and Mored'.

MABBOTT, T. O. 'Chatterton and Milton: a Question of Forgery', *N&Q*, 177 (28 Oct. 1939), p. 314.

> An investigation of the possibility that some marginalia in a Bible, previously ascribed to Milton, might be by Chatterton.

——————, 'Chatterton's *Execution of Sir Charles Bawdin*', *BN&Q*, 1, No. 1 (1935), p. 9.

> Seeks information regarding the two title-leaves, one with the imprint of Newbery and the other with that of Goldsmith, in *The Execution*, 1772.

——————, 'Landor on Chatterton and Wordsworth: Marginal Notes', *N&Q*, 156 (9 Mar. 1929), pp. 168-69.

> Landor's comments on the Chatterton section of Howitt's *Homes and Haunts of the English Poets*.

——————, 'A New Poem By Thomas Chatterton', *MLN*, 39 (1924), pp. 226-29.

> Manuscript of an unfinished and previously unpublished poem entitled 'Elegy Oct. 29 [1769]' in the Phoenix Collection of the Columbia University Library, with reference to the 'Elegy to the Memory of Mr. Thomas Phillips, of Fairford'.

——————, 'Notes on Chatterton: a Poem Attributed to Him', *N&Q*, 174 (19 Feb. 1938), p. 133.

> A reprint of an unsigned poem in the collection of the Pennsylvania Historical Society, possibly by Chatterton.

——————, 'Notes on Chatterton: an Uncollected Poem', *N&Q*, 174 (15 Jan. 1938), pp. 45-46.

> A six-line unfinished poem, in a hand resembling that of Chatterton, the text of which is here printed.

——————, 'Two Letters of Thomas Chatterton in America', *N&Q*, 160 (7

Mar. 1931), pp. 170-71.

> Notes on the manuscripts of two letters in the collection of the Pennsylvania Historical Society: 'For Mr. James Dodsley' and the postscript of a letter which the poet sent to his mother from London in 1770.

MEYERSTEIN, E. H. W.　'The Authorship of "The Auction"', *TLS*, 12 May 1921, p. 308.

> Meyerstein attributes the poem to Chatterton on the basis of a mention in the poem of Barrett and Burgum.

—————————, 'The Authorship of "The Auction"', *TLS*, 9 June 1921, p. 373.

> Further quotations from 'The Auction' are compared with other works by Chatterton. Meyerstein mentions poems not in any printed edition.

—————————, 'The Authorship of "The Auction"', *TLS*, 11 May 1922, p. 308.

> Further proof of authorship is deduced from the special usage of the word 'waddle' which is found elsewhere in poems known to be by Chatterton with the same unique meaning.

—————————, 'Chatterton: a Correction', *TLS*, 16 July 1925, p. 480.

> Identification of the author of *Poems, Consisting of Tales, Fables, Epigrams &c., &c. by Nobody* (London, 1770), in which three pieces are given to Chatterton, as James Robertson.

—————————, 'Chatterton and the Kilburn Priory', *TLS*, 30 July 1938, p. 507.

> Seyncte Godwin, supposed by Dean Milles to be a fictitious title, is identified by Meyerstein with one Godwin, the founder of a hermitage at Kilburn.

—————————, 'Chatterton and the *Oxford Magazine*', *TLS*, 31 May 1923, p. 371.

Mention in Chatterton's pocket-book under the date 3 May 1770 of 'Mr. Coote in the Oxford Magazine' leads Meyerstein to believe that a number of Chatterton's works may be found therein.

MEYERSTEIN, E. H. W.   'Chatterton's Birtha', *TLS*, 18 July 1936, p. 600.

An investigation of Chatterton's debt to *Gondibert and Birtha*, by William Thompson.


——————, 'Chatterton, Coleridge and Bristol: 'The Sacred River'', *TLS*, 21 Aug. 1937, p. 606.

Coleridge's debt to Chatterton is shown by parallels between the African Eclogues and 'Kubla Khan', viewed against the geography of Bristol and district.


——————, 'Chatterton: His Significance Today', *in* Royal Society of Literature, *Essays by Divers Hands*, 16 (1937), pp. 61-91.

The effect of Chatterton's environment on his poetry and the influence of his poems on the later Romantics is discussed. The evaluation of his significance today is slight.


——————, 'A Chatterton Manuscript', *TLS*, 27 Dec. 1947, p. 675.

Records the aquisition by the Bristol Library of a manuscript of Chatterton's lines to Michael Clayfield, differing from the British Library's autograph MS. and the version transcribed by George Catcott as printed in *Works* (1803).


——————, 'Chatterton's Spelling of 'Aella'', *TLS*, 4 Feb. 1932, p. 76.

A history of the spelling of the name from Anglo-Saxon times. The poet began with 'Ella' but seems to have preferred 'Aella' up to the date of his first correspondence with Walpole.


——————, 'De Quincey's Copy of Chatterton's *Miscellanies*', *TLS*, 8 May 1930, p. 394.

Meyerstein records De Quincey's notes in an imperfect copy of Chatterton's *Miscellanies in Prose and Verse*, 1778.

MEYERSTEIN, E. H. W.    'The Forged Letter from Peele to Marlowe', *TLS*, 29 June 1940, p. 315.

       A forged letter that appeared in the *Annual Register* for 1770, p. 107, under the title 'Anecdote of Shakespeare never printed in his Works'. Meyerstein, noting similarities between phrases used in the letter and those employed by Chatterton in the Rowley Poems, attributes the authorship of the letter to the Bristol boy poet.

——————, 'Lydgate and Chatterton', *TLS*, 16 Apr. 1925, p. 268.

       Meyerstein points out similarities between lines in Chatterton's verses by John Lydgate on Rowley's 'Songe to Aella' and those in Tottel's edition of Lydgate's *The Fall of Princes* (IX, 2245 *sq.*).

——————, 'Poems by Chatterton in Dodsley's *Annual Register*', *TLS*, 21 July 1921, p. 468.

       Mentions 'The Auction' and other poems in the *Annual Register* for 1769. Three unsigned poems in Chatterton's satirical manner in the *Register* for 1770: 'The Poet and Straw. A Fable'; 'The Two Kings. A Fable'; 'On Our Modern Comedies'.

——————, 'A Satirical Eclogue by Thomas Chatterton', *TLS*, 2 July 1934, p. 488.

       Eighty-two unnumbered lines from a sheet in the British Library collection of Chatterton's MSS. are here given consecutively and entirely for the first time.

——————, 'Wordsworth and Chatterton', *TLS*, 21 Oct. 1926, p. 722.

       Wordsworth's enthusiasm for Chatterton, especially in his use of meter.

MILLER, F. S.    'Thomas Chatterton's Historic Sense', *Journal of English Literary History*, 11 (June 1944), pp. 117-34.

       'Chatterton's historic sense . . . is unique in being spontaneously generated rather than acquired from training and travel, in resulting from and in a mediaeval dream world.'

MONTGOMERY, H. R.   'Chatterton and the Rowley Poems' in *Famous Literary Im-postures, a Series of Essays* (London: E. W. Allen, [1884], pp. 1-38.


MUIR, P. H.   'A Chatterton Edition', *TLS*, 5 Apr. 1941, p. 172.

> Reply to R. W. Chapman (*BN&Q*, 1, No. 2 (1935), p. 8), that both title leaves of *The Execution of Sir Charles Bawdin* (1772) were printed together, separated and inserted in copies of the work.


NORTHUP, C. S.   'Gray and Chatterton', *Mark Twain Quarterly*, 5 (Spring 1943), pp. 17-18.

> Northup contrives to see similarities between Chatterton and Gray that simply do not exist; to say that the Rowley Poems were in-spired by Chatterton's association with Mary Redcliff Church while Gray's 'Elegy' drew the same inspiration from a church at Stoke Poges is an overstatement of the obvious.


POTTER, G. R.   'Thomas Chatterton's 'Epistle to the Rev. Dr. Catcott'', *MLN*, 39 (June 1924), pp. 336-38.

> The poem is Chatterton's reply to Alexander Catcott's *Treatise on the Deluge* (1761; rev. 1768) and reveals the boy's belief that the Scriptures could not be interpreted literally and that God works entirely through natural law.


POWELL, L. F.   'Thomas Tyrwhitt and the Rowley Poems', *RES*, 7 (July 1931), pp. 314-26.

> Powell shows that when Tyrwhitt undertook to publish the Rowley Poems, he was still a believer in the authenticity of them.


RUSSELL, A. H.   'The Amazing Boy. Poetry of Thomas Chatterton', *WDP*, 5 and 21 Apr. 1924.

> Notes on Chatterton's poetic genius, with various quotations.


SALMON, ARTHUR L.   'Chatterton', *Poet-Lore*, 4, No. 12, pp. 593-99.

Chatterton's potential rather than his achievement is the source of his reputation. Salmon maintains that the boy's genius is evident only in the Rowley Poems.

SCUDDER, H. H.  'Chatterton on Money', *N&Q*, 195 (22 July 1950), pp. 323-24.

A comparison of Chatterton's 'Of the Auntiaunte Forme of Monies, Carefulli Gotten for Mayster William Canynge by Mee Thomas Rowleie' with the section devoted to money in Camden's *Remaines* (1657), a book written after the time of Rowley and before Chatterton.

SECUNDUS APOLLO (PSEUD.)  'Criticisms on the Language of 'The Bristowe Tragedie'', *MMr*, 15 (Jan. 1803), pp. 14-16.

The author points out verbal parallels and similarities between Chatterton's 'Bristowe Tragedie' and the popular song 'Old Towler', Shakespeare's *Richard III*, *Hamlet* and Gay's *The Beggar's Opera*.

SKEAT, W. W.  'Chatterton's Knowledge of Anglo-Saxon', *N&Q*, 4th ser., 7 (1 Apr. 1871), pp. 278-79.

Some examples analysed, with the conclusion that 'Chatterton knew no more Anglo-Saxon than he might have picked up in an hour from a glossary'.

——————————,  'Essay on the Rowley Poems; with an Explanation of the Plan of the Present Edition', in *The Poetical Works of Thomas Chatterton*, v. 2; Bell and Daldy, 1871.

A study of rhyme and meter and an analysis of the pseudo-antique language.

STAUBERT, PAUL.  *Thomas Chatterton und seine Rowley-Dichtung, Untersucht auf Grund der Psychologie Reifezeit.*  (Bonn: Hanstein, 1935).

Reviewed in: *Anglia Beiblatt*, 48, pp. 49-50; *Archiv für Studium neueren Sprachen*, 169, pp. 137-38; *Literaturblatt für germanische und romanische Philologie*, 7, pp. 174-77; *Die neueren Sprachen*, 45, p. 378; *Zeitschrift für neusprachlichen Unterricht*, 36, p. 55.

STEEVENS, GEORGE,   'Origin of a Modern Image in Chatterton's 'Excelente Ballade of Charitie'', *MMr*, 10 (Sept. 1800), pp. 149-50.

> Steevens believes that the line 'For the *horse-millanare* his head with roses dighte' in the 'Excelente Ballade of Charitie' was suggested to Chatterton by the sign over a sadler's shop which read 'A Horse Milliner'.


SYPHER, F. W.   'Chatterton, Coleridge and Bristol', *TLS*, 28 Aug. 1937, p. 624.

> Takes Meyerstein to task for publishing details in an article of 21 August, p. 606, which Sypher had discovered and intended using in his own publication. Points out inaccuracies in the Meyerstein article.


——————,   'Chatterton's African Eclogues and 'The Deluge'', *PMLA*, 54 (Mar. 1939), pp. 246-60.

> Passages in the African Eclogues which resemble those in 'Kubla Khan', and a discussion of the possibility that both poems owe something to the Reverend Alexander Catcott's 'Treatise on the Deluge'. The latter work is compared in detail with the Eclogues.


TAYLOR, DONALD S.   'The Authenticity of Chatterton's *Miscellanies in Prose and Verse*', *PBSA*, 55 (1961), pp. 289-96.

> Distinction between Bristol and London pieces, with doubt thrown on most belonging to the later period.


——————,   'Chatterton: the Problem of Rowley Controversy and its Implications', *PQ*, 46 (1967), pp. 268-76.

> Taylor sees three phases in Chatterton's development: 'the poetic apprenticeship followed by four dormant years, the Rowley period, and the last year's sustained drive for poetic, Grub Street, and political notoriety, with its Bristol and London sub-cycles'.


TILLOTSON, GEOFFREY,   'Warton's Last Words on Rowley', *MLR*, 35 (Jan. 1940), p. 62.

Corrects H. P. Vincent's article by naming the author of the unpublished letter as Thomas Wharton, a friend of the poet Gray,
and not Thomas Warton, the author of *The History of English Poetry*.

**TING, NAI TUNG.**   'The Influence of Chatterton on Keats', *K-SJ*, 5 (1956), pp.
103-08.

Attempts to supplement, not to contradict, Gitting's observations
on the influence of Chatterton on Keats' poetry.

**THOMAS, P. G.**   'Fresh Light on Chatterton', *Welsh Outlook*, 16 (June 1929),
pp. 182-84.

The first entire printing of Bishop Percy's letter to Lord Dacre,
dated 6 September 1773, giving the opinion that the Rowley MSS.
were spurious.

**VINCENT, H. P.**   'Warton's [*sic*. Wharton's] Last Words on the Rowley Poems',
*MLR*, 34 (Oct. 1939), pp. 572-75.

Cites unpublished letter in the Theatre Collection, Harvard College Library, revealing echoes of much later work in the language
of the Rowley Poems.

**WATKIN-JONES, A.**   'Bishop Percy, Thomas Warton and the Rowley Poems, 1773-
1790', *PMLA*, 50 (1935), pp. 769-84.

Contains the full text of Percy's report to Lord Dacre on the two
Rowley MSS. sent to him by Dacre for examination; and a letter
from Sir Robert Chambers to Bishop Percy explaining his failure
to deliver the MSS. to Dacre, and Percy's reply to Chambers.

**WEBER, CARL A.**   *Bristols Bedeutung für die englische Romantik und die deutsch-
englischen Beziehung*.  (Halle: Max Niemeyer Verlag, 1935).

Prominence given to Chatterton.

**WELLS, CHARLES.**   'Chatterton Again', *BT&M*, 31 May 1924.

Chatterton's genius defended against Arthur Salmon's view that
his work is dead.


**WERKMEISTER, LUCYLE.** 'The First Publication of Chatterton's Verses 'To Miss
C. On Hearing Her Play on the Harpsichord'', *N&Q*, 207 (July 1962), pp. 270-71.

> Points out that the first publication of these verses was not, as
> is generally thought, in Edward Gardner's *Miscellanies in Prose
> and Verse* (Bristol, 1798), but in the London magazine *The World*,
> on 22 September 1792.


**WHITE, ERIC W.** 'Chatterton and the English Burletta', *RES*, n.s., 9 (1958),
pp. 43-48.

> Kane O'Hara's *Midas*, when performed at Bristol in 1768, inspired
> Chatterton's fragmentary burlesque 'Amphitryon'. Material from
> the latter was later used by the poet for *The Revenge*.


**WRIGHT, G. W.** 'Chatterton Set to Music', *N&Q*, 157 (14 Sept. 1929), p. 190.

> Discussion of a catalogue entry in the Chapter Library of St.
> Paul's, of some verses of Chatterton set to music by Richard
> Clarke, the MSS. of which had not been identified.


——————, 'Chatterton Set to Music', *N&Q*, 171 (26 Sept. 1936), pp. 228-
29.

> Identification of the MS. mentioned in *N&Q*, 157, p. 190.

WORKS OF IMAGINATION

[ANON.]   'The Death of Chatterton', in *William Tyndale, and Other Pieces*. (Bristol: J. Wright and Co., 1895).

      The poem appears at pp. 29–46.


A. D.   'The Death of Chatterton', *Bath and Bristol Magazine*, 2 (1883), No. 4, p. 453.

      A poem submitted after reading a biographical sketch of Chatterton in volume 1 of the *Magazine*.


ANDERSON, ROBERT.   *Complete Edition of the Poets of Great Britain*. (Edinburgh: Mundell and Son, 1795; volume 11).

      Selected verses by Preston, Pye and Haley at pp. 295*ff*.


BELL, NEIL.   *Cover His Face: a Novel of the Life of Thomas Chatterton*. (London: Collins, 1943).


BLAIKIE, JOHN A.   'Ode on the Death of Thomas Chatterton', in *Love's Victory: Lyrical Poems*. (London: Percival and Co., 1890).

      Poem at pp. 69–81, beginning: 'List, list, O placid stream!'.


BLAU, HEINRICH.   *Thomas Chatterton: Tragödie in vier Akten*. (London: Hirschfeld Bros., 1887).

      An idealised picture of Chatterton; historical facts are disregarded, *e.g.* the action is set in 1756!


CARY, THOMAS.   'Elegy to the Memory of Mr. Thomas Chatterton, late of Bristol', *Town and Country Magazine*, 2 (1770), p. 551.


COLERIDGE, SAMUEL TAYLOR.   'Monody on the Death of Chatterton', in *Rowley Poems*, ed. Lancelot Sharpe (Cambridge, 1794).

This original version of the 'Monody' appears at pp. xxv-xxviii. A revised text was printed in *Poems on Various Subjects* (Bristol, 1796), pp. 1-11. For discussions of the history of the 'Monody', see: I. A. Gordon, 'The Case History of Coleridge's 'Monody on the Death of Chatterton'', *RES*, 18 (1942), pp. 49-71; C. G. Martin, 'Coleridge, Edward Rushton, and the Cancelled Note to the 'Monody on the Death of Chatterton'', *RES*, n.s., 17 (1966), pp. 391-402 and 18 (1967), p. 174.

COTTLE, JOSEPH. 'Epitaph for a Proposed Monument to Chatterton, at Bristol', in *Malvern Hills*, 4th. edition. (London: T. Cadell, 1829).

> The 'Epitaph' is at p. 169 and begins: 'Pause, Stranger! this recording marble bears / The name of Chatterton!'.

CURNICK, THOMAS. 'Ode on the Death of Chatterton, Written at St. Vincent's Rocks, at Clifton, near Bristol', in *Jehosaphat, with Other Poems* (Bristol: M. Bryon, 1815).

> The 'Ode' is at pp. 104-07.

DALLAWAY, JAMES. *Sonnets to an Aeolian Harp; on the Death of Chatterton.* (Privately printed at his Press at the Fort, 1788).

> The 'Fort' here referred to is probably Rodborough Fort, which was purchased by Dallaway's father in 1787.

DANE, CLEMENCE (PSEUD.) 'The Marvellous Boy. A Sketch.', *The Listener*, 6 Feb. 1941, pp. 201-02.

> The writer was Winifred Ashton.

EASTMEAD, JOHN S. 'Chatterton: A Poem', in *Poems* (Bristol: William S. Matthews, 1843).

GRATTAN, FRANCIS W. *Thomas Chatterton, the Marvellous Boy, in the Foes and Woes of a Poet.* (Persia, N.Y., 1918).

> A four-act drama.

HEADLEY, HENRY.   'Ode to the Memory of Chatterton', in *Fugitive Pieces* (London: C. Dilly, 1785).

> The 'Ode' is at p. 76, beginning: 'Ill-fated Youth, was thine breast / Where fell Despair might fix her dark resolve'.


IRELAND, S. W. H.   *Neglected Genius. A Poem; Illustrating the Untimely and Unfortunate Fate of Many British Poets: From the Period of Henry the Eighth to the Area of the Unfortunate Chatterton.* (London, 1812).

> Pp. 57-127 and 144-51 relate to Chatterton.


JAHN, HANS HENNY.   'Thomas Chatterton. Eine Tragödie', *Spectaculum*, No. 2 (1959), pp. 267-333.

> See: H. H. Jahn, 'Zur Tragödie 'Thomas Chatterton'', *Sinn und Form*, Beiträge zur Literatur, 6. Jg., Hft. 516, pp. 805-09.


JAMES, JOSEPH.   'Lines, Written After Seeing in the Exhibition Room, in Broad-Street, the Model of a Monument to the Memory of Chatterton, by a Lady' *and* 'Lines, On Seeing the Picture of the Dying Chatterton Exposed for Sale in a Broker's Shop, Close Beside his Monument', in *Poetry* (Bristol: John Taylor, 1841).

> The first poem, consisting of twelve six-line stanzas, is at p. 128; the second is at p. 131.


KRUGER, RAYNE.   *Young Villain with Wings. A Novel Based on the Life of Thomas Chatterton.* (London: Longmans, Green and Co., 1953).


L. M. S.   'The Grave of Chatterton: A Poem', *Mirror of Literature, Amusement, and Instruction*, 7 Dec. 1844, p. 379.


LACY, ERNEST.   *The Bard of Mary Redcliffe.* (Philadelphia: Sherman and Co., 1910).

A five-act play of 205 pages, limited to 350 copies; illustrations, one of which is from Henry Wallis' painting of Chatterton.

LACY, ERNEST, 'Chatterton: A One-Act Play', in *Plays and Sonnets* (Philadelphia: Sherman and Co., 1900).

A limited edition of 200 copies. The play is at pp. 1-28. The frontispiece shows an etching of Julia Marlowe as Chatterton.

LANGFORD, JOHN A, 'A Pilgrimage to the Birth-Place and Grave of Chatterton', in *Pleasant Spots and Famous Places* (London: 1862).

MATHIAS, T. J, *Rowley and Chatterton in the Shades: or, Nugae antiquae et novae. A New Elysian Interlude, in Prose and Verse.* (London: T. Becket, 1782).

Reviewed in: *MR*, 67 (1782), pp. 235-36.

MEYERSTEIN, E. H. W, 'Chatterton at Shoreditch: a Sonnet', *BT&M*, 24 Aug. 1929.

Chatterton prepares for death: 'Methought I saw him on the plasterer's bed'.

—————, 'Chatterton in Holborn: A Vision', *English*, 2 (1948), No. 37, pp. 19-20.

—————, *Redcliff Hill. A Colloquy in one Act.* (Bristol: G. H. Holloway, 1948).

A conversation between Sarah Chatterton (the poet's mother), Mary Newton (his sister) and George Catcott. Reminiscences of Rowley and Chatterton centred on the theme of Mrs. Newton's letter to Dr. Glynn, 20 February 1790. Limited to 100 copies.

MONTGOMERY, JAMES, 'Chatterton: Stanzas on Reading the Verses Entitled 'Resignation', Written by Chatterton, a few days before his Melancholy End', in *Poetical Works*, vol. 2 (London: Longman, *et. al.*, 1841).

>The poem, dated 1802, is at pp. 152-53 and begins: 'A dying swan of Pindus sings'.

OWLETT, F. C. *Chatterton's Apology; with a Short Essay on Blake, and a Note on Cowper.* (Hoddesdon, Herts.: Thomas Knight and Co., 1930).

>An imaginary conversation between Chatterton, Burgum, the pewterer, and Horace Walpole. The scene: An Unfrequented Spot without the Circuit of Elysium.

PENZOLDT, ERNEST. *Der arme Chatterton: Geschichte eines Wunderskindes.* (Leipzig: Inselverlag, 1928).

>A novel broadly based on Chatterton's life. Translated as *The Marvellous Boy*, by John J. Trounstine and Eleanor Woolf (New York: Harcourt, 1931).
>Reviewed in: *Zeitschrift für französischen und englischen Unterrichten*, 28, p. 229; *Die neue Rundschau*, 40, pp. 428-29.

R. F. 'Elegy on T. Chatterton, or the Boy of Bristol', *GM*, 58 (Dec. 1788), p. 1106.

>Eighteen four-line stanzas, including the Epitaph (2 stanzas).

ROBERTS, WILLIAM I. 'Chatterton, or The Mynstrelle. A Fragment', in *Poems and Letters* (London: Longman, 1811).

>The poem is at p. 56.

ROBINSON, MARY. 'Monody to the Memory of Chatterton', in *The Poetical Works of Mary Robinson* (London: Richard Phillips, 1806).

>The 'Monody' is in volume 1, at p. 246.

ROSSETTI, DANTE GABRIEL. 'Thomas Chatterton: A Poem', in *Collected Works* (London: Ellis and Scrutton, 1886).

>The poem is in volume 1, at p. 337.

**SASSOON, SIEGFRIED.**  *On Chatterton: a Sonnet.*  (Winchester: Blakeney, 1930).

> The Sonnet begins: 'If I could stand in byegone-centuried shoes'. The MS. of the poem was lent to E. H. Blakeney, the printer, by T. J. Wise, who had found it among the author's letters to Sir Edmund Gosse. The printing was unauthorised. Limited to 14 copies.

**SIMARA (PSEUD.)**  'Chatterton: a Poem', *Bristol Observer*, 26 May 1860.

> A thirteen-line poem on the death of Chatterton, signed 'Clifton, 15 May 1860'.

**SHERIF, S.**  'Sonnets on the Poet Chatterton', *Oddfellows Magazine*, 9 (Jan. 1846), p. 39.

**SOUTHWOLD, STEPHEN.**  'To Chatterton', in *The Common Day* (London: G. Allen and Unwin, 1915).

**SUSMAN, H.**  'Chatterton. An Echo', *McBride's Magazine*, 81 (1908), pp. 251-53.

> A short story in which the narrator believes he is Chatterton reincarnated.

**THISTLETHWAITE, J.**  'An Elegy, to the Memory of a Young Man lately deceased', *Gentleman's Museum and Grand Imperial Magazine*, No. 5 (Nov. 1770).

> Discovered by Meyerstein (see: *TLS*, 8 Feb. 1934, p. 92).

**TYLER, FROOM.**  'The Sleepless Soul', *Bristol Evening World*, 20 Nov. 1935.

> Described as 'a sentimental satire', these are scenes from a radio play, broadcast on Tuesday, 28 March 1935, depicting the last hours of Chatterton's life.

**VIGNY, ALFRED DE.**  'Chatterton', in *Oeuvres Complètes*, ed. F. Baldensperger (Paris, 1964).

See: C. W. Bird, *Alfred de Vigny's 'Chatterton': a Contribution to the Study of its Genesis and Sources* (Los Angeles: Lymanhouse, 1941).

WHITEHEAD, CHARLES.    'The Death of Chatterton: a Poem', in *The Amaranth*, ed. T. K. Hervey (London: A. H. Bailey and B. B. King, 1839).

YEARSLEY, ANN.    'Elegy on Mr. Chatterton', in *Poems on Several Occasions* (London: G. G. J. and J. Robinson, 1787).

The 'Elegy' is at pp. 145–49.

# INDEX

Chambers, Sir Robert, 113
Chapman, John, 81, 82
Chapman, R. W., 33, 102, 110; *Cancels*, 39*n.*
Charles I, *Eikon Basilike*, 13
Chatterton, Sarah, poet's mother, 120
Chaucer, Geoffrey, 83, 104; *Canterbury Tales*, 36*n.*
Clark, F. E., 94
Clark, Sally, 96
Clarke, Sir Ernest, *New Lights on Chatterton*, 102
Clarke, Richard, 114
Clayfield, Michael, 108
Cole, William, 49
Coleridge, Samuel T., 17, 67; *Kubla Khan*, 108, 112; *Monody on Chatterton*, 17, 58–59, 117; *Poems on Various Subjects*, 118
Collins, William, 81
Colston's Charity School, 21, 105
Columbia University Library, 106
*Contemporary Review*, 96
Cooper, Elizabeth, *Muses' Library*, 23, 101
Coote, J., editor of *Oxford Mag.*, 108
Cottle, Basil, *Thomas Chatterton*, 102
Cottle, Joseph, 56, 66, 76; *Malvern Hills*, 118
*Critical Review*, 41, 48, 51, 75, 76, 77, 78, 84, 85
'Crito', 79
Croft, Sir Herbert, 17, 66*n.*; *Love and Madness*, 17, 48, 61, 66*n.*, 67, 76
Crofts, Thomas, 36
Cromek, R. H., *Remaines*, 15*n.*
Cunningham, Allan, 14*n.*
Curnick, Thomas, *Jehosaphat*, 118
*Current Literature*, 91

Dacre, Lord, 113
Dallaway, James, 54; *Sonnet*, 118
Dampier, Henry, *Remarks*, 76
Dane, Clemence, *pseud.*, 118
Davis, Bertram R., 94
Davis, John, *Life of Thomas Chatterton*, 89
Dean, F. R., 94
Dennis, Leah, 102
De Quincey, Thomas, 108

Devonshire, Duchess of, 67
Dix, John (George Spencer Phillips), *Life of Chatterton*, 89, 97
Dixon, W. M., *Chatterton*, 23*n.*, 102
Dodsley, James, publisher, 93, 107, 109
Domesday Book, 79
'Donation of Constantine', 13
Drury-Lane Theatre, 62
Dryden, John, 23
Ducarel, Andrew C., 81, 82
Dyer, George, 62

Eagles, Thomas, 33
Eastmead, John S., *Poems*, 118
Edgcumbe, Richard, 103
*Edinburgh Review*, 18*n.*, 70
Egerton, John, 62–63
*Elegy Oct. 29*, 106
*Elegy to Thomas Phillips*, 106
*Elinoure and Juga*, 104
Elizabeth I, 80
Ellinger, Esther, *Thomas Chatterton*, 20, 21*n.*, 22, 89
Elrington, Stephen N., *Life and Character of Thomas Chatterton*, 89; *Martyrdom*, 90
*Englischen Studien*, 92
*English*, 120
*English Review*, 78
*Epistle to the Rev. Dr. Catcott*, 110
Eschenburg, J. J., 104
*Études Anglais*, 105
'Eugenio', 81
*European Magazine*, 51, 65, 75, 79
*Excelente Ballade of Charitie*, 112
*Execution of Sir Charles Bawdin*, 102, 106, 110, 111
*Exhibition, The*, 20, 21, 89

Farrer, James Anson, *Literary Forgeries*, 103
Fell, Isaac, 94, 95
Fielding and Walker, publishers, 46
*Foreign Quarterly Review*, 19, 101
Forman, H. B., *Thomas Chatterton and His Latest Editor*, 103
*Forum*, 105
*Freeholder's Magazine*, 45, 94, 95
Freudian psychology, 22
Fry, John, 41
Fry, Dr. Joseph, 102
Fry, Dr. Thomas, 33

130